The Importance
of Being Musical

The Development and Practice of a Music Curriculum

by

Cynthea A. Frongillo

Published by:

The Association of Waldorf Schools of North America
3911 Bannister Road
Fair Oaks, CA 95628

The Importance of Being Musical
THE DEVELOPMENT AND PRACTICE OF A MUSIC CURRICULUM

Author: Cynthea A. Frongillo

Editor: David Mitchell

Proofreader: Nancy Jane

Cover design: Hallie Jean Bonde

Cover photograph: Aliki Sapountzi

ISBN # 1-888365-17-X

Curriculum Series

The Publications Committee of AWSNA is pleased to bring forward this publication as part of its Curriculum Series. The thoughts and ideas represented herein are solely those of the author and do not necessarily represent any implied criteria set by AWSNA. It is our intention to stimulate as much writing and thinking as possible about our curriculum, including diverse views. Please contact us with feedback on this publication as well as requests for future work.

David S. Mitchell
For the Publications Committee
AWSNA

Table of Contents

Foreword

In the sculptural, pictoral realm we look at beauty, we live it, whereas in the musical realm we ourselves become beauty.

In music man himself is creator. He creates something that does not come from what is already there, but lays a foundation and firm ground for what is to arise in the future.

Rudolf Steiner
Practical Advice to Teachers

This small book has grown out of fifteen years' experience in teaching music in Waldorf schools. I did not have formal training in music, but rather I was asked by my colleagues to teach music in my first year of class teaching simply because I loved to sing, could already play the recorder, and did both reasonably well.

I learned by doing — at first I discovered mostly what not to do — and developed ideas that worked, refining them over time. It was an amazing discovery for me to experience how the pedagogical indications given by Rudolf Steiner were borne out in the music lessons, and frustrating to see how little the advice given for scheduling the music lessons could be put into practice consistently, since it had to be weighed against so many other demands put on a comprehensive school-wide schedule. Singing lessons directly after recess are certainly difficult but often happen because of time constraints. Yet, I have begun to feel that music is the single most important gift we can give to our children.

Building up an adequate music program takes many years. To have a chorus and orchestra of six, seventh and eight graders who can sight-read adequately, skills must be built starting in the second and third grades, an ethos must be created among the students so that they look forward to being in the school orchestra, and teachers must be found who can carry and direct all the different areas involved in a music program over many years.

Unfortunately, music teachers are often the most ephemeral members of a school faculty, and in my experience, it is one area in which emergencies frequently arise. Because musicians often live just on the edge of poverty (a picture of music's place in modern society) and are so dependent upon part time work in many different venues, they are the most likely to leave a school when financial necessity makes it imperative. Suddenly, someone must be found to do the strings, often someone with no knowledge of Waldorf education; accompanists come and go at some schools with the seasons. Frequently, very skilled and talented musicians who have little experience with children and no classroom management skills are drafted from the community.

For an area of life which is so important, there are often scant resources to spare to build up the instruments and materials needed for an adequate music program. This book is also a plea to teachers and faculties to give this tender and sensitive area of the soul's education the space and time it needs to grow.

I offer this booklet to my colleagues in a spirit of collaboration. To new teachers suddenly landed with music lessons, to experienced music teachers stepping newly into Waldorf teaching, and to those who have been "doing the music" in their schools for years, this is addressed, not as a manual or as the way to teach music, but rather as an opening to a conversation. These are things which have worked for me in my lessons and why I have found them useful. They are open to amendment; in fact, I am constantly finding new things, or finding that something which worked with one class is definitely not right for another. In this spirit I open the dialogue on music teaching in a Waldorf school.

Introduction

People of ancient times perceived that the cosmos was alive with musical tones. Gazing up into the night sky undimmed by our modern lights, radiant with stars and the wandering, ever-changing planets, they saw the homes of their gods and of their own souls, the source of all musical experience. When they spoke to their gods in prayer, they sang, for they knew that they had come from a world imbued with musical tones. We, too, as Steiner's clairvoyance has revealed, revisit the world out of which our spiritual and physical being was formed each night in our sleep consciousness, although today that consciousness is dimmed and unavailable to us in our waking life. There the world of color and tone is spread out before us in all its immense beauty, as the beings of the cosmos go about their sublime business. It is this awesome vision which we carry back into our daytime existence as the dim memory which is earthly tone and harmony. It is this deeply submerged remembrance of wonder that makes us hearken in the street to a beautifully sung tone by a street musician, or to a passing fragment of Mozart heard in the jangle of modern urban life.

It is this memory which today we stand in danger of losing, surrounded as we are by so much noise and "unmusical" music. I do not mean to condemn the earnest striving of modern composers. Obviously the course of historical musical development has many twists and turns yet to make. We are a long way still from experiencing the musical depths of the single tone in a way which Steiner predicted would be ultimate musical experience yet to come, although anyone who feels the discords of modern compositions would certainly agree that we have arrived at the half-tones. This path of development, however, has certainly led us as a musical culture down some very dead ends. Our adolescent children especially are subject to a media which has lost all appreciation of melody and harmony. Just at the age when they need so badly to find ideals, the ideal of true music, even in its coarse physical garb, is often unavailable to them in popular culture. It is imperative for their very souls that we as Waldorf teachers find a way to give the children in our care a connection, however imperfect, with the purest examples of tone, melody, and harmony, as an antidote and counterbalance to the purely mechanistic rhythms in which they are immersed by MTV.

No matter how sensitive to nature and music we remain as adults, we have lost much of the magical experience of childhood. Young children, however, live very much in the imaginative realms of music and magic. This is a realm attainable to us adults only in dreams, whose rapidly changing moods and events are never surprising to us, and which carry something of a musical element transposed into a realm of images.[1] In our dream life we inhabit a world similar to that of a child immersed in a fairy story, in which people who suddenly understand the language of animals and the song of the birds, for example, do not seem extraordinary or fantastic.

That music is, in fact, a language is apparent to us as adults only after much thought. To a child who sings for the joy of singing, music is as vital as speech. If words are the food and substance of the growing power of thought in the young child, music is the nourishment and the expression of the world of feelings and imagination, of the soul. It is, too, the rhythm of life and of movement, something easily forgotten in these days when the rhythm of work songs has been replaced by the personal CD player. For this reason music is of vital importance in the education of the young child. It is just in the early years that a sensitive nature can be fostered and developed. Teaching the young child music gives him/her a language without words, a language of emotive expression which will stand him/her in good stead during the turbulent years of puberty, when a flood of feelings too powerful, new, rich, and strange can be given outlet and expression in musical practice, and can find an echo in the music of those like Mozart and Beethoven and more modern masters who have found a way to the same tumultuous and sublimely beautiful places in the soul.

Music is the one art form which lives only in the moment of its performance. Unlike the art of painting, sculpture, and architecture, where the artist can go away when the work is finished, a human being is needed in every moment to allow music to live in time. The better the musician, the more transparent she is to the music itself. The results of a composer's efforts are not the piles of manuscript he or she has written, but the music that can be made from them. Even when recorded, it is temporal, or temporary, and to be heard again, it must always be recreated. The practice of music is a constant schooling of discipline and imagination. Let the mind wander, and the tone falters, losing its anchor in the inner experience of music. The moment the attention is diverted, rhythm breaks its steady underlying pace, and the music fails. The fact that children have a healthy love of music is an opportunity and a door to teach so much that is necessary for their lives. The understanding itself of music is beneficial in ways that Steiner points out again and again in his leacures to teachers: *"To help the children to become aware of a structure in a melody works wonders for their development."* [2]

Music can be appreciated on every level, and it is the product of every culture, however sophisticated. It carries meaning in its lyrics, but itself has laws and measure and patterns which provide a source of serious study to any scholar. Even the structure of a scale is formed according to laws and measure, and in this sense the realm of music is akin to a landscape of a sort, against which the melodies and rhythms we hear arise and fade away again.

Rudolf Steiner stresses the importance of music even beyond the term of our life on earth. Music is the last thing we retain after death as a memory of earthly life, and that memory leads over into the cosmic sounding of the music of the spheres in the world of the soul.[3] In fact, we are made of music, for the proportions of our very skeleton are built up of musical intervals.[4] The young child builds up his nerve organization as a musical instrument in the early years of life:

What is experienced musically is really man's hidden adaptation to the inner harmonic-melodic relationships of cosmic existence out of which he was shaped. His nerve fibers, ramifications of the spinal cord, are marvelous musical strings with a metamorphosed activity. The spinal cord culminating in the brain, and distributing its nerve fibers throughout the body, is the lyre of Apollo. Upon these nerve fibers the soul-spirit man is "played" within the earthly sphere. Thus man himself is the world's most perfect instrument; and he can experience artistically the tones of an external musical instrument to the degree that he feels this connection between the sounding of strings of a new instrument, for example, and his own coursing blood and nerve fibers. In other words, man, as nerve man, is inwardly built up of music, and feels it artistically to the degree that he feels its harmonization with the mystery of his own musical structure.[5]

Truly, to take the opportunity to teach children to re-member music is as important as any other teaching they will learn in a Waldorf school.

Music in the Life of a Waldorf School

Waldorf schools include the introduction of all the arts as an integral part of the child's life. While some other schools, pinched for funds, would exclude an art course here or there, Waldorf schools are dedicated to integrating all the arts more and more fully into every area of study. While his thoughts and observations about music are scattered throughout his many lecture courses, Steiner's indications for music in the classroom are an outline only, usually simply noting when a given element should be introduced. He expected all the teachers to use their imagination and love for the children as guides in their education.

In a Waldorf school, music forms an integral part of almost every lesson: as a means of gathering the kindergartners into a circle in the morning, in a main lesson on numbers in the first grade, in geography lessons in the upper grades, in language lessons, and, of course, in music lessons themselves. In the lower grades, the teacher will often sing "Good Morning" to the class, and they sing it back to their teacher joyfully, in a first experience of the day of listening and echoing a pure tone. As attendance is taken, the individual child waits for her name to be sung by her teacher, and sings out her presence in the class, thus giving the teacher another answer to the question, "How is it with this child today?" Nearly every class begins the day in song, which awakens the children, coming each from their different homes to the presence of their classmates around them in a harmonious way, getting them all "on the same wavelength" and breathing and sounding in unison. Each class from the first grade on also plays music on the recorder as a part of that same morning "circle," and day by day the children's awareness and control of their growing bodies, control of breathing, dexterity, and coordination are enhanced along with their burgeoning skill on the instrument.

All Waldorf schools emphasize music for the reasons I have indicated above, and each class studies it as a regular part of their daily or weekly routine. The study of music should be an integral part of the curriculum of a Waldorf school, and it should be the aim of every school to have an established orchestra and a good chorus, both in the lower school and the high school, with the majority of the students able to understand, read, and appreciate music individually and together. Such goals are only possible with the determined intentions and backing of the faculty as a whole at every stage. There are numerous failings and pitfalls along the way; these are to be expected and must be taken in stride. To build a good music program takes years.

Our music making is a gift to the children of our schools. In the moment, it is a joy to them (some seventh graders in the midst of puberty might take temporary exception to this), but it is like a magical charm in a fairy tale, too, for further along on their journey, they will discover that it is a means of self expression in the midst of their emotional trials and celebrations, as well as a basis for relationships with others, a thing of beauty and wonder for their whole lives. Rudolf Steiner stated, "Music makes us truly human."

Live vs. recorded music

It should be noted at the outset that, ideally, music in its study and performance is always live in a

Waldorf school. The performers, whether they be professional musicians who come to play for us or the children themselves, are an integral part of the musical experience. None of us as teachers would record the spoken content of our main lesson and play it for our class! If, as Steiner says, and as musicians have constant evidence, the echoes of the spiritual world as well as the soul of the performer live in the music she plays, giving the children a recorded version of a piece of music, no matter how good the quality, is only a mechanical experience.

The children learn early on the decorum necessary for a concert, and their listening over the years to the various classes playing and singing gives them a real appreciation for the skill and practice needed to give a good performance when it is their turn on stage. In a complete Waldorf school there are many opportunities when the children are able to play for each other, and visiting musical performances from the wider community around the school should be welcomed wherever possible. In addition, the children themselves need outlets for performances in more formal settings, although arrangements are often complicated for outside performances, and other lessons must be sacrificed. It always seems self-evident to me that the children should be able to take an afternoon excursion to perform for a new audience on the other side of town. The protest of the language teachers reminds me how caught up we are as teachers in our own realms, in spite of our active striving to work as a community. That said, of course one's job as the advocate for music in a faculty is to argue mightily for these events, for they are a vital part of the music curriculum!

As we listen to and watch another speak or sing, dance or play, we accompany the movements of the other with our own etheric gestures. Our larynx is active in listening; we dance inwardly when listening to music. It is this intimate activity of our own that makes the other fully understood and brings us into sympathy. We can be enriched and ennobled by an accomplished and sensitive concert performance. We even say such an experience is "uplifting." Accompaniment is an activity that we all engage in at every performance.

This inner activity is quite absent while listening to a recording. Although our feelings may be very much involved, the particular consciousness of the performer is engaged elsewhere, not even present during our experience. As teachers we know the effect of giving directions or instructions without our full consciousness (I hope I am not the only one guilty of this from time to time!). The content of our words is ignored, followed half-heartedly or not at all, and to repeat this again and again would weaken our effectiveness as teachers. How much harm is done by giving the children a musical experience without consciousness, or even presence? It may be argued that the children hear recorded music all the time, but such a fact only emphasizes that as teachers we must strive to give them an experience of living music whenever possible.

The use of recorded music must be carefully considered and its effects weighed against its benefits. It is possible to play recorded music for study purposes. In an older choir, for example, one can play several different examples of a choral work that the children have been practicing. A musically mature group will be well able to listen critically, noting the dynamics, attack, phrasing, and qualities of voice and should be able to incorporate improvements based on this analysis into their own performance. This analysis is recommended, in fact, for its own sake, regardless of whether a recording is used. For geography lessons, one could introduce musical idioms and styles from distant lands if it is not possible to find a native musician, or if the music is beyond the skill of the class teacher. A biography of Beethoven would be meaningless without a demonstration of his music (although it would be much better if such a study were timed to coincide with a local concert to which the children were to be taken afterward). One might introduce recorded music as an example for theoretical study, or for practice in following a score, but only as an introduction to an avenue or study which the class would then follow in application. Of course, in the Music History Block in the high school, a good CD player is essential. One could not ask an orchestra to oblige by playing the opening to Beethoven's Ninth several times while the class commented on the structure of the movement! The important thing to remember is that any such study will have a heavily intellectual element, since it is only the notes and their relationships that is heard, nothing of the presence of the musician striving to bring the music into being. I could not recommend such a thing for classes younger than grade seven.

Musical experience and technique:
singing and instrumental music

Music teaching is a broad subject and takes on many different aspects as the children progress through the grades. There is a coherent thread to be followed, but to go year by year through the music curriculum may be confusing. To avoid a too scattered approach, I will first try to give a brief overview, and then I will take the two areas of singing and instrumental lessons separately. At the end of the book, there is a sample curriculum, year by year. I offer this as a model only, to be changed and adapted by any school's and teacher's individual circumstances, talents, and resources.

An Overview

The teaching of music as a subject in itself branches into three areas. The first is singing a capella involving at first simple songs in which the children imitate the teacher. This evolves in time into rounds, then part-singing. In this area, one stresses accurate listening, beautiful and pure tone production, and the accuracy of intervals leading eventually to sight singing with all the mastery this entails. Since singing comes so much more naturally to children (those who struggle for months to move their fingers on the recorder in imitation of the teacher can often sing beautifully), it is in this realm that the introductory steps into notation and theory are best made in grade four.

With instruments, technical skill is the aim. The classes begin right away in the first grade with the recorder (at first a specially-made pentatonic instrument) and play purely by imitation for several years. The children can be introduced in the third grade to playing the lyre and later to the violin as a class experience. (It is best if notation is not introduced until the fourth grade.) Instrumental playing in the early grades involves training the breathing and the hands, and developing the technical aspects of the particular instruments. Instrumental playing is able to utilize and practice with each new instrument the focus on hearing and tone, which has been developed earlier in singing

Exercises in rhythm are pursued in the Waldorf schools for their own sake and for a variety of reasons. One of our most important tasks as class teachers is to help the child to establish a relationship to the rhythms of heart and lungs in a healthy way. This, of course, includes a mandate for the music teacher, but it goes beyond the scope of the music lessons in the early grades and is pursued in main lesson as a part of the morning circle. Expansion and contraction in moving forms, form drawing, and in the changing moods in the lessons contribute to this in every lesson of the day. Counting rhymes and patterns are also practiced each morning for the sake of the mathematical rhythms, which then develop into the times tables. How helpful for the future music teacher are the morning-circle activities of the first grade class teacher on the three and four times tables! It is possible later to ask a fourth grade what "number" is in a piece of music that they have learned, and they can answer immediately, "That song has four in it!" The rhythm and control of the breath, the clapping and poetical rhythms pursued by the class teacher as aids in developing memory and coordination — all are taken up and developed further in the conscious study of music in the later grades.

Singing through the Grades

Since my own teaching involves mainly singing, I will include some sources and music for the lower grades, and some of the exercises and practices I have found to be successful. I would like to say at the outset that these are things which have worked for me, and that there are certainly other ways of introducing and teaching music to be found within the Waldorf school movement. Each teacher must find his or her own material in order to inspire and teach. The exercises that follow might be a start for any more inexperienced music teachers who are perhaps daunted by a task which can become truly a joy and a labor of love.

There is one requirement which must be mentioned with great emphasis for any teacher who sings with his/her class. The best music teacher is in reality a student. The new teacher who has been asked by his/her colleagues to sing with the lower grades may feel inadequate, as well may the seasoned veteran. Our voices are a very personal and intimate expression of our inner nature. Perhaps one may feel that others sing "better than I do," and are, therefore, embarrassed. Then, too, another may feel secretly that "My voice is really very beautiful. Of course they asked me to sing with the second grade." The needful thing for any singing teacher is not that one's voice at the moment be "good" but that one has an imagination for how it might be better. Anyone who is striving and wrestling with one's voice to attain a purer tone and has an imagination of what pure singing is as an inspiration will do well.

In singing for the children, one must remember the deep penetration of the child into his or her sense impressions. The class will imitate **very** well what they hear and see and sense. This includes the way in which the teacher sings, what she imagines as her ideal voice, her inner mood, and her expression. The reverence felt by the teacher for the voice, this gift of the gods to us, will be evident in the class without ever mentioning a word about it. It works even to the most subtle levels. I have on several occasions taught my children a song in which I was not sure of a particular interval, having sung the piece only a few times before the lesson. On each occasion, although I sang it correctly for them while they learned it, the children stumbled for weeks over just that particular interval whenever we sang the tune! I mention this here because it points up the importance of the inner experience of the teacher in attaining a pure imagination of the music, and musical tone is here most important.

While there are many examples of singing styles around us to imitate, the one which serves the children we teach best is one in which the personality is suppressed, so that each tone can sound as purely as possible. Even if your own voice is not "good," the children will sense your striving and will aim for that same quality for which you are aiming. Since the class will be your class for many years, your ability and theirs will grow together. They will also, by the way, serve as your "mirror," and you can get a good idea of how you are progressing, even if you cannot change your voice very easily, by listening as your classes sing. Too heavy a quality in their voices, and any tendency to shout, or to sing too loudly is an indication that you as the teacher and example are doing something wrong. A silvery, light-filled tone and a class that sings happily, even without the teacher's prompting in moments of transition, or while out playing in the yard indicates that you are on the right path.

Training and education for the teacher

There are several excellent books available to the teacher on singing and improving one's vocal quality. The most thorough is Valborg Werbeck-Svardstrom's *Uncovering the Voice*, which was written out of years of experience and intensive work in singing, and with the help and advice of Rudolf Steiner. The other book is *Singing and the Etheric Tone* by Dina Winter. While it is possible to work independently with these texts, it is, of course, best to have a singing coach in these methods. Special care must be taken in choosing a singing teacher from the world of performance music. Many singers and teachers use a physiological method which causes unnecessary stress and emphasis on the physical means of voice production, i.e. the larynx and the breathing, and ignore the imaginations and the mental preparations necessary to produce a tone which is close to the ideal.

If there is no anthroposophical vocal teacher available, a classical voice teacher would be best. Begin to develop a critical ear by listening to singers in performance, and see if you can hear the differences in their voices. Modern singing methods utilizing jazz, pop, and folk styles, which emphasize and bring out the breath and the personality, are to be avoided.

By far the best way for any teacher to advance in overall musical training is to join a chorus or choir which meets regularly and performs fairly frequently. The thrill and wonder of being a part of a great choral work, bringing it into being in community with conductor, orchestra, and your fellow choir members is the very experience of joy which we are trying to instill in our students. For a busy teacher, the time out of the week taken up by chorus practice might be unthinkable. "I already go to the faculty meeting, and the college, and the monthly parent council meetings. How can I give up *two or three hours* of a week-night and then take the extra time for rehearsals just before a performance?" Yet after a busy day at school wrestling with one's schedule, colleagues, meetings with parents, and the general complications of modern life along with preparation of one's lessons, an evening given over to singing Bach's *Christmas Oratorio*, or Handel's *Messiah* is balm to the soul. For the class teacher, the resulting education in listening, reading, and musical judgment, guided by a competent conductor is excellent and will bear fruit every time you play part-music with your class. For the music teacher it is an indispensable and ongoing part of your training.

It might just be possible to rescue the music heard on recordings for the purposes of studying the melodies and thematic structure of a piece. This more intellectual exercise would be pursued in the high school. Melody does live in the head , as anyone who "can't get a tune out of my mind" will attest. Although Steiner has a different intent in the following passage, he does stress the importance of melody (and, therefore, melodic analysis) and its connection with the thinking. At any rate, the following is certainly worth quoting for its own sake:

The element of melody guides the musical element from the realm of feeling up to that of thinking. You do not find what is contained in thinking in the thematic melody, but the theme does contain the element that reaches up into the same realm where mental images are otherwise formed. Melody contains something akin to mental images, but it is not a mental image; it clearly takes its course in the life of feeling. ...The significance of the element of melody in human nature is that it makes the head of the human being accessible to feelings. Otherwise, the head is only open to the concept. Through melody the head becomes open to feeling, to actual feeling. It is as if you brought the heart into the head through melody. In the melody you become free, as you normally are in thinking; feeling becomes serene and purified. All outer aspects are eliminated from it, but at the same time it remains feeling through and through.

Rudolf Steiner
The Inner Nature of Music and the Experience of Tone

Singing in the Lower School

And just as man experiences the inherent nature of music, so the forms of his body are shaped out of music itself. Therefore, if the teacher wishes to be a good music teacher he will make a point of taking singing with the children from the very beginning of their school life. This must be done; he must understand as an actual fact that singing induces emancipation; for the astral body has previously sung and has brought forth the forms of the human body. Between the change of teeth and puberty, the astral body frees itself; becomes emancipated. And out of the very essence of music emerges that which forms man and makes him an independent being. No wonder then that the music teacher who understands these things, who knows that man is permeated through and through with music, will quite naturally allow this knowledge to enrich the singing lesson and his teaching of instrumental music. This is why we try not only to introduce singing as early as possible into the education of the child, but also to let those children with sufficient aptitude learn to play a musical instrument so that they have the possibility of actually learning to grasp and enter into the musical element which lives in their human form, as it emancipates and frees itself.

Rudolf Steiner
Human Values in Education

Kindergarten

Very young children are bound up with their surroundings in a way we cannot remember without great effort, and, indeed, in a way we can hardly fathom. With all their senses they engage the world around them, bringing the sights and sounds into themselves with the same hunger they have for physical nourishment. And like the effects of the foods they eat, their surroundings, the moods, and the visual and aural stimuli in which they pass their time will do them either good or ill. How much responsibility we have, therefore, to see that these defenseless children are exposed to only those things which will help them to grow in a healthy way!

The Waldorf kindergarten is a warm and harmonious world, one in which the teacher sings softly to initiate new activities and stories. The children join her with pleasure and learn new songs by imitation, songs which are connected with the season or with some particular activity or task. They experience the happy cacophony of play, hammering, building and shouting, and its opposite, the harmonious and melodic introduction to the more structured and solemn story time as a rhythmic breathing. Music has its place as an integral part of the children's life. "When man takes speech back into song, he moves closer to the realm of pre-earthly existence from whence he was born into earthly conditions. It is human destiny that man must adapt himself to earthly conditions with birth. In art, however, man takes a step back, he brings the earthly affairs surrounding him to a halt; once again he approaches the soul- spiritual element from which he emerged out of pre-earthly existence. "[8]

In Rudolf Steiner's indications for children of this age, he recommends using the "mood of the fifth" as the characteristic gesture of the melodies for the children. He encouraged the use of songs in the pentatonic mode, but with a specific aim in mind. The child, he said, floats in a dreamlike way through the waking hours, having not yet made that step into individuality which comes with such a painful jolt in about the ninth year. Young children live in the world of the kindergarten and the first years in the classroom like a bubble in the sea — undifferentiated in mood from their surroundings. The songs we sing with them, he said, should have that same floating quality, and, therefore, we should use melodies which have no "do" note, no ground, and no particular key. This is quite a challenge in composition for the teacher, but I wish to stress that, to my mind, this is the reason for restricting ourselves to the pentatonic tones. Many of the songs one finds in a pentatonic songbook are simply in a minor mode and have just as much a "do" as does Beethoven's *Fifth*! What is important is that we use melodies which do not always come down onto the "do" note (the note which is the same as the key signature of the piece) at the end of every phrase or verse. The song should not "come home." The melody should rise instead and end on a fourth or a fifth. If possible, the teacher should compose songs with this dreamy, floating quality. Once made up, however, I advise you from experience to write them down, for they are very hard to remember! We are so used to "landing" on a reference note in modern songs that this type of melody does not stay in our minds easily. "Floating" songs like this can be incorporated into the fairy tales one tells the class or can be made part of the morning circle, and the children will learn them much more easily than any adult, for they do not yet know anything about cadences or keys. It is impossible to restrict oneself to this type of tune, however, and folk tunes, work songs, and seasonal songs are used in the kindergarten and the lower classes constantly. Whatever the song, the melody should be stressed, keeping the voice as high and smooth as possible, and emphasizing the rhythms, if that is desired, with gestures. This would go a long way toward fulfilling Steiner's indications to keep the children from incarnating too deeply by means of the tones.

The teacher of young children, whether male or female, should use a high, silvery tone in singing and encourage the children by example, never by specific direction unless someone is really being a rascal, to sing softly and fluidly. These are the first artistic breathing lessons in the child's school life. To embrace a line of melody with the breath and to feel its movement upwards and down with grace and feeling, following their teacher as s/he moves about the kindergarten is a wonderful foundation in musicality.

First Grade

In first grade, singing continues as a threshold, bridging one activity with another in a more structured way. Each lesson, whoever the teacher, usually begins with a song or two. In main lesson, the first one of the day, the verses and songs emphasize the time of year, the approaching festival, the stories under consideration in the lesson block as a whole. The children's names are sung by the teacher in taking attendance, and the children are encouraged to sing back their responses. Rhythm is used in both song and verse, although its chief purpose in these lower grades is to enhance the memory and aid with developing coordination, rather than to gain musical understanding. Still, the teacher might initiate a clapping game in which the children must answer the tapping of a bird on the window or some such thing. The children enjoy such games and stories in which they can take part. These and the rhythm exercises used in the morning circle are the seeds which develop later into a conceptual understanding of musical rhythm and notation later in the fourth and fifth grades. The ability to imitate and answer a rhythmic pattern in clapping is, in fact, one of the signs of first grade readiness in a Waldorf school.

Class teachers who have particularly low voices (this can include women as well as basses) should ask another teacher, preferably a soprano, to sing with their classes once a week or so. If upon listening to the class singing, one detects any tendency to shout, this is because they are singing with their "speaking voice" and not really singing at all. It is possible to correct this tendency simply by pitching all songs high enough so that the children cannot speak at that pitch. If your voice sounds better at a lower pitch, remember that it is the ideal voice that your class will imitate, not necessarily your own timbre. Most will, however strive to imitate your pitch.

Depending on the class, there will be a number of children who cannot do this. Their voices will meander in very different directions, or perhaps just climb onto a note and stay there, no matter where the song goes. This is to be expected in a large class. If there are five or six "growlers" in your class, and you are especially sensitive, this will make your music making more of a trial, but it is best to ignore it at this age. The children themselves are mostly unaware of it, and many so-called "tone deaf" children will straighten themselves out over the first few years of school. It is important not to call attention to these children in any way in the class, and if other children notice it, to make light of it. (A recent comment heard in the fourth grade was that, "He has a crooked voice!") Working with such children at a later age can be successful, but the attempt must be made when the child is old enough to understand why s/he is being singled out. A voice is the most intimate expression of one's inner being. Intervention like this must be done with great warmth and sympathy. I would wait until grade four, at least, before gently taking such a child aside. At the and of the book there a few indications as to how this might be done. (See appendix B.)

I have had experiences while leading singing groups at conferences and the like which I am sure are not unique. Many times individuals have approached me after an initial session with a mood almost verging on desperation. As children they had been told that they could not sing by a thoughtless sibling, their friends, or, horrible though it seems, by a music teacher! Since that time, right into adulthood, they have not sung with confidence. Many have not sung at all. I listen to them privately, and there is usually no problem with their voice, or their intonation. Having been singled out in a thoughtless moment by another in this way as a child has crippled their ability to make music right into adulthood. In courses designed to help "non-singers" begin to sing, people are frequently moved to tears when they discover that they do have a voice and can learn to use it to make music. To take away another's divine birthright to sing is surely a terrible crime.

Presenting a song

When introducing a new song, I always give a little story about it. Perhaps it is a song about a little squirrel. One should characterize the animal, tell a funny little anecdote about a squirrel that you have met, or actually tell a story in which an event in the song figures. This introduction will engage the attention of the whole class, if you should happen to have one or two children who "don't like to sing." After the story or the introduction is told, the teacher should sing it, the whole song, as clearly as possible. If, as is often the case, the song has a chorus, usually by the time they have heard it through once, they are eager to sing along with the part that repeats after each verse. If there is no chorus, then teach it phrase by phrase. I sing the first phrase several times, stopping at a logical place in the tune, and by the second time, most of the class is singing along with me. We then proceed, phrase by phrase in this way until we have sung the whole song. Then we sing the whole song several times. In most schools, the first years of singing are done with the class teacher. If the singing is to be done with a special teacher, for a first music lesson, one needs at least two or three songs and their introductions in one's pocket!

I always try to ensure that the songs I teach have some connection with the children. I do this by means of the stories I tell, or by some game that is connected with the song, or by letting them work on a picture out of the lyrics of a song I have taught them. One can also use seasonal songs that the class teacher may not have used in class. The use of chimes or a lyre or harp occasionally as accompaniment to their singing deepens the children's experience and provides a "mantle" of sound into which they can sing. The children must be engaged in what they are singing. This draws them into themselves and helps them to live into the inner quality of music. It fosters the mood of reverence which is so important (although this doesn't mean that there must be no laughter in a music lesson!) and helps them to remember the melody and the words.

  " . . . There is something that should really be present in the child at a higher stage, this feeling of well-being at the inward flow of sound. Imagine what would happen if the violin could feel what is going on within it! ...If the violin could feel how each string vibrates with the next one it would have the most blissful experiences, provided, of course that the music is good. So you must let the child have these little experiences of ecstasy, so that you really call forth a feeling for music in his whole organism, and you must yourself find joy in it.
  "Of course one must understand something of music. But an essential part of teaching is this artistic element of which I have just spoken."[9]

  I would caution the teacher against too many "childish" and cute songs. There is enough trivia around them in the media, and the music lesson is a time for real music. If one is able to introduce appropriate songs properly, the children will love to sing them. If a light mood is desired, there are plenty of folk tunes which are fanciful in their content and yet not sentimental.

First indications of pitch

It would be good to begin already in the first grade to indicate the pitch by the movements of one's hand. This needs no explanation, but many in the class will begin to imitate the motions, and it will help the class to sing along with you, for they will soon begin to know that up means that the melody is going to go up with the next note, and down means a drop in pitch. If, as a special teacher, you have a whole period to fill dedicated to music, give each child a book in which to make pictures of the songs as you teach them. Their pictures can be quite free, and some will choose one aspect of the story of a song, some another. This ensures a quiet period at the end of each lesson, and the class will enjoy having this record of all the songs they know.

Experiencing the sounding tone

One must use one's imagination to introduce children to singing and listening exercises in the early grades. The images and movements of the teacher must inspire the children to imitate the way the teacher sings. Since the experience of tone is such an important part of singing, one could begin by describing some beautiful sound you have heard, and how you would love to hear it again. Ask the children how well they hear. Can they hear the sounds outside the classroom? Can they hear the neighbor's cat meowing? Can they hear the grass growing? What is their favorite sound? Can they hear while you bring into the room a sound from the stars? Ask them to sing you a song they have learned from their class teacher. Can they sing it so softly that it might make the frightened little mouse that you saw the other day feel better?

I have told a young class a story that I will gladly share with other teachers as an example, for what it is worth. I was walking one spring day through the New England woods when I came upon a hedgehog that was sunning himself on the top of an old stone wall. I don't know why he didn't hear me approach- he must have decided that he needed just a little more of his winter's sleep. I share that feeling thoroughly every morning and felt instant sympathy with him. I froze, hating the thought that as soon as I, the intruder, made him aware of my presence he would rush for cover, and I would lose this moment of (perhaps quite one-sided) intimacy with a wild creature. What to do? Dear reader, I sang. Very softly at first, and as I approached I sang louder and was pleased to see the hedgehog slowly rouse himself and look around contentedly for a while. Then, after a direct look at me, he stretched and shambled off clumsily into the woods. (Perhaps I chose the wrong song. I am probably the only person who can say with scientific certainty that hedgehogs don't care for *Amazing Grace*.) At any rate, it is the quality of the voice being just as much a part of nature as the song of the birds that I wished to bring to the class by means of this story. Such an anecdote is enough to introduce a singing tone or a simple tonal pattern that one could ask the class to imitate as a first singing exercise.

All these activities could be part of a music lesson, a necessary part if a whole forty minute lesson is scheduled for music in the first or second grade. To keep children singing for a full forty minutes would be inviting disaster, for singing has an exhilarating effect upon small children, and the stories and book work will help to contain them and also provide the "breathing-in" at the end of a period of singing. If singing is combined with recorder, of course, the recorder playing, with its necessary concentration on the fine motor skills, will provide that, too.

Second Grade

The Waldorf curriculum stresses the value of stories of saints and fables and legends which provide the music lessons with a rich source of melodies and lyrics. Many early Gaelic songs have just the mood earlier described as ideal for young children, are pentatonic, and go beautifully with the material taught in second grade. The *Oxford Book of Rounds* is a good source of little songs- even the bawdy rounds have good, easily learned melodies, and the words can be changed. The songs are done in unison, of course, in the first and second grades, and even through most of the third. Using these simple rounds as material in the lower grades gives the class a delightful surprise later on when they find that many of the songs they know can be sung as rounds!

The first rhythm exercises

I usually begin in grade two to count into a song, letting the class experience the beat of the measure without too much explanation. Clapping exercises continue as imitation. After several months, one can introduce a means of recording the rhythms used. I have developed a way of describing the rhythms with a series of words describing the sounds in nature. After telling a simple story – perhaps, even a scene I saw on the way to school when the sun had come suddenly and disappeared behind a rain cloud, I draw several pictures on the board and ask the class to tell me what they are. I use the following words, without showing or indicating the time values of the words, although I will do so here for clarity: "Sun (a quarter note), "Rain-Drop" (a pair of eighth notes), "pitter-patter" (four sixteenth notes splashing into a puddle), and for triplets a buttercup. If the teacher draws these simple pictures on the board in a series and points to each picture using a steady beat, the children will say them over and over again. One can interchange the pictures in different combinations, and you have the children's first rhythm exercises! I would recommend introducing this towards the end of second grade, just as something fun to do. It should be worked on much more intensively in third. (See singing exercise 1.)

Sun,   Sun,   raindrop, Sun, raindrop,   Sun, raindrop, sun.

A singing exercise for the early grades

Second grade children enjoy a challenge, so several singing exercises can be introduced. My classes have especially liked one that we called a "ribbon of tone." The teacher first brings the picture of the beautiful sky-dome of blue over head, then gives an example of a single tone floating down like a ribbon from the sky, coming from above and behind as it draws near, and sings it as purely and as softly as possible. The sound is increased until the room rings, then it fades away and floats back into the sky and the room is silent again. The children are then invited to join their voices to the teacher's, giving them the imagination that the sound produced approaches from above and behind and must be no wider than the ribbon. One thus can work with refining their tone and pitch, getting it more and more of a uniform quality. In higher grades, one can continue this using with two or more tones in harmony, practicing the intervals with a metamorphosis of this same exercise. One can then speak of a braid of gold and silver, or sun and moon light.

Notation in pictorial form

　　In the second grade, work with the gestures indicating melody continues; I have used a particular song for months before showing the children the "secret" of what I am doing. It is good to have a song about hills for this, for when one day you walk along the front of the class while describing the melody with your hand, the children will discover that you are making a picture of the song! Done with chalk against the board, the hills of the lyrics emerge visibly in front of them. Once you have shown them this, the children will want to draw all the tunes they sing, and will usually be eager to know what each new melody "looks like." About half-way through the year, one can take this a step further. Using the very first song I drew for them, which was about a tired pony going up and down a hill, I now describe how slippery the hill was, for it had suddenly begun to rain on the way home. The poor pony only felt safe when he stepped onto the solid stones along the way. I draw the stones on the road, and at the whole note, I draw an especially large stone, outlined only, because at this place there was enough room for him to stop and rest awhile. Then we sing the song again, and the children see how at that point in the song, the rhythm does indeed stop and rest on the long note. This sort of imagery makes sense to the children.

The music for this picture is found in the back of the book. (See singing exercise 2.)

It is interesting to note that recent research in standard science on the ways in which the brain "comprehends" music has found that the part of the brain activated when discriminating between differing pitches is the precuneus, the same as that which is active in interpreting visual imagery.[10] The instinctive feeling that a "C" is "high" is associated with the gestures one makes to indicate its location in a visual, spacial sense. It is "up there" in the same way a cathedral spire is "up there." The interpretation of melody visually is quite a natural development for the lower grades, provided the imagery used is imaginative and appropriate to their age.

Occasionally, one will have a class in which a few of the children already are familiar with ordinary music notation. They enjoy being able to say, "I know what that is! It's a whole note!" Those who are familiar with music from private music lessons take obvious satisfaction in knowing something more than their classmates. One must acknowledge this, and then one must eventually show the entire class, briefly and without much fuss, what the proper notation looks like. It is important not to make a mystery of this. In my experience, the entire class then goes back very happily to the more imaginative way of working with pictures.

At the end of the second grade, I introduce the diatonic scale as a singing exercise at the start of each lesson. This is the usual major scale, known by its pitch names: do, re, mi, fa, sol, la, ti, do.

Some musical games

One game children at this age especially like to play involves the gestures, by now known very well to the children, which imitate the rise and fall of the melody with the hands as we sing. One child is elected to go out of the room while the rest of the class and the teacher choose a tune the class knows very well. The child is then brought in again, and the entire class shows the melody silently, the rising and falling of the pitch indicated with their hands. It is important, of course, that they do this accurately; the teacher can stand behind the elected child and "dictate" the movements while the class mimics the teacher. If the child can recognize the tune, he or she gets to choose the next child to go out. This can also be done with clapping the rhythm of the song.

All the while, the class is learning more and more fully developed melodies and songs. While the pentatonic songs which are taught in main lesson in the language arts block as an accompaniment to the stories told in class are especially beautiful, the teacher must not be shy about making his or her own songs, particularly if they are also to be used as material for recorder playing. It is easy to do if one only has courage, especially since the range of notes is at first limited on the pentatonic recorder. Try choosing a poem you like, or writing one suited to the class, then let your fingers wander on the recorder until you find a suitable and pretty melody. Write it down quickly, before you forget it! (Again, this is experience speaking. I have left a good many lovely songs behind in my wake, sure that I would easily be able to remember them for tomorrow's lesson.) It is especially important to teach the class the recorder music as songs first, so the children connect their finger movements on the recorder with the rise and fall of the melodies they already have experienced as song.

Frequently, one is tempted to introduce the class to the singing of rounds towards the end of the second grade. There are all of those wonderful rounds which they have been singing in unison waiting to be explored! Even if your class is "musically precocious," I would recommend against this. It is a great strain on them to hold a part against their classmates. Even if you yourself sing the second voice against the whole class, most of the children will be concentrating so hard on their part that they will not even hear the beauty of the harmony. The sight of some children singing doggedly with their fingers in their ears so they do not get thrown off track by listening to something different should be enough to tell you that it is too soon!

Third Grade

The major and minor third

... If we really want to reach the child, the cultivation of his musical understanding must commence with an understanding of the fifth. This is the really important point. And then we can give great benefit to the child if we approach him with the major and minor moods and a general appreciation of the third in this connection when he has passed the ninth year and begins to ask important questions. One if these important questions is expressed in the urge to live with the experience of the major and minor thirds. This occurs round about the ninth and tenth year and should be particularly encouraged.[11]

This is the year in which the children are introduced to the diatonic recorder, and the year in which they will experience fully the major and minor third. This is a giant threshold in the development of the child.The "nine year old change" is dealt with pedagogically in many books and lectures and is a frequent subject of discussion in child studies. It is beyond the scope of this small book to emphasize it in all of its pedagogical implications. There is an important musical step that children make as they cross the threshold out of the Garden of Eden, however, that must be stressed. In the earlier grades, the children are still dreaming into music, and the ideal music remains somewhat unfocused and "floating";

the content of the songs you do with them are filled with imagination and pictures. While that is still the case, now one can begin to emphasize the interval of the third (do- mi).

Steiner described the effect of the larger intervals of the fourth and fifth (do- fa, and do- sol, respectively) as an experience of being outside the body, not incarnated fully, which is why he so strongly recommends them as suitable intervals for the younger children. With the change of consciousness of the nine-year old, the children experience themselves alone within their bodies for the first time, with all the naughtiness, wonder, and grief that this entails. For reasons that will be apparent, it is best to wait to introduce the first conscious experience of a song in the minor mode until the first Old Testament Block is finished. Through the experience of the major and minor third, one accompanies the child in his/her experience of the expulsion from paradise and guides the child into an inner mobility, the reassurance that inner and outer are both states in which the child can find a home. This is the essence and substance of the music lessons in the third grade. Steiner speaks of this change with reference to the spiritual development of mankind as a whole in a pair of lectures called *The Human Being's Experience of Tone*, given to teachers and eurythmists. If I may be indulged in a more theoretical excursion, I will quote most of the relevant passages here:

Now why is it that we today experience the interval of a third?...Previously in experiencing the fifth, man had been inclined to say: The angel in me is becoming a musician; the muse speaks in me. It was not yet right to say: I sing. This is not possible until the interval of a third is experienced. When this happens one can begin to experience oneself as the one who sings. ....During the time of the fifth, major and minor had no meaning. One could not even speak of them yet.

Major and minor, so remarkably bound up with human sub-
jectivity, with the real inner life of feeling in so far as this is
linked with bodily existence, begin to appear during the fourth
post-Atlantean epoch and are connected with the experience of
the third interval.[12]

It is of interest to note that in the distant spiritual history to which Steiner sometimes refers, it was not
the intervals, compressed into one octave which we experience today. What is referred to as the "mood of the
fifth" in ancient times was in fact the experience of no
interval smaller than the fifth! This means that if we were
truly to attempt to reproduce that experience, we would
need very different instruments than are available to us
(an interesting project for someone to attempt). Since
most of us are limited to a range of about an octave and a
half, this would restrict our singing to only four notes!
Steiner describes an earlier period in Lemurian times in
which the "cosmic third" was experienced. (This is the
first human experience of what comes as a western musical development, a recapitulation in historical times in
the Renaissance as the harmony of the third.) He calls
this early experience of the third which occurred in ancient times an "objective" third. That is, the C of one octave and the E of two octaves higher (C - E).

Because man in ancient times was able to have a direct
experience of intervals which we describe today as the tonic in
one octave, the second in the next octave, and the third in the
third octave, he was able to perceive a sort of objective major
and minor; not a major and minor experienced within himself
but a major and minor expressing a feeling of what the gods
experienced in their souls.....We cannot describe what man in
the Lemurian age experienced by any such names as joy and
sorrow, exaltation and depression; we must say that through

this particular musical perception in Lemurian times when he was quite outside himself in perceiving these intervals, he experienced the cosmic jubilation of the gods and the cosmic lamentation of the gods. We are able to look back to a time on earth really experienced by man when what is experienced today as major and minor was, as it were, projected out into the universe. What today flows through his emotion and feeling was then perceived by him outside his physical body as the experience of the gods in the cosmos. What must be characterized as our present inner experience of the major mood was experienced by him outside his body as the cosmic jubilation, the cosmic music of the gods rejoicing in their creation of the world. And what we know was experienced in Lemurian times as [the minor third was] the vast lamentation of the gods over the possibility of what is described in the Bible as the fall of man, the falling away of mankind from the divine spiritual powers, the powers of good.[13]

Thus, the introduction of songs in the minor modes is an important threshold for the nine year old child and rightly belongs with the story of the fall in the Old Testament.

In *The Human Being as Music*, Lea van der Pals describes the moods of major and minor as follows:

The human being produces notes from no other source than out of pleasure or pain. Either one feels drawn out of oneself in the experiencing pleasure and sends the note after the soul, streaming out in order to halt it – it is notes in the major which sound outwards – or one feels oneself compressed by pain and searches to give the tormented soul a way out; it is notes in the minor which break forth from the suffering, seeking to release the pressure.[14]

I once had the experience of playing music with a woman who was severely handicapped. As a hysteric, she was completely at the mercy of her surroundings, and her responses to stimuli were violent and immediate. There was a harp in the room, and I sat down to play some chords and intervals for her. Upon hearing open fifths (without the third) and fourths, Louise was calm, expectant, and gave me a running commentary on her inner life. " I like that! That's nice." As soon as I played the major third (do, mi, sol) in the chords, she began to laugh! For as long as I played the major chords she was ecstatic, almost lifting out of her chair to go dancing about the room. A minor cadence brought all this to an instantaneous halt. Louise was in tears within seconds, so distressed that she was in danger of doing herself harm. "I don't like that! I'm unhappy! That's making me sad!" Deep sobs wracked her. Alarmed at this, I instantly went back to the open intervals I had played at first, and her calm demeanor returned.

Louise was pathologically sensitive to these intervals. She underwent immediate soul transformation, entirely subject to the power of music playing over her soul. But children are naturally sensitive to all that we bring to them in terms of music.

A first presentation in class

I like to introduce the minor third to a third grade by asking them to tell me, as Louise did so naturally, what their feelings are upon hearing it. I am always awed by their responses. Usually the time for this falls around Michaelmas. I use a beautiful French round to which I set the words of a Michaelmas verse. "Children, I am going to sing you a new song that we will learn. It's different from most of the other songs we have sung so far. I want you to listen to it and tell me in what way it is different, if you can." Then I sing the song as beautifully as I can. Sometimes the children ask to hear it again. Then

I ask them, "What did you feel while you were listening?" I have had answers like, "It feels like we are floating like stars, all alone." One or two children will say it sounds sad, but usually someone in the class can be more specific: "Not sad, really, but serious, like in a church." One child said, "It feels as if you are singing to someone who has gone far away, and you cannot reach them. It's lonely." Another felt the melody had come "from the stars."

I then give them the words minor and major, and tell them that this song is in a minor key. I have not explained the mechanics of the minor scale, but simply left it as an experience, to be taken up later in the fourth grade. I have found that over a short time, the class develops an ability to recognize immediately whether subsequent songs are major or minor. One can point out, or, better still, get the children to observe, how the minor third feels constricted, smaller, different from the major third, which is so full of confidence and light. After a while in your characterizations of major and minor you can show the class what some very familiar songs sound like when they are sung in the minor mode. "Row, Row, Row your Boat" is a good one. The transposition into minor brings observations such as, "It must be raining." "I bet they are rowing upstream." "They sound like they don't want to go!" The class enjoys this and are always amused to hear happy songs they know sung with the minor third in place of the major third.

One more example of the evidence of this musical threshold can be given here. In the occasional concerts we have at our school, when visiting musicians come to play for us, and when we have been invited as a school to attend the children's concerts given downtown, I have noticed something over and over again. The pieces played are usually classical- the purpose is, after all, to acquaint the children with orchestral pieces. Since the program is intended for children, usually works in the major keys are chosen. The children sit attentively, listening happily to the sounds of all the instruments blending together. But when a piece in a minor key has been selected for variety the younger children in the audience begin to fidget almost immediately. This is not naughtiness, for even the very good children move about restlessly and must be chided. I realized after observing it many times that it is because, not yet having crossed this nine-year old threshold, the young child has nowhere to "put" the experience of the minor third. Music simply has not yet drawn into them, and their inner life cannot hold the experience.

Singing exercises; beginning the lesson

As the year progresses, one can begin singing exercises which occupy the first ten or fifteen minutes of every singing lesson from now on. Major scales can be sung. I have my classes sing up and down a scale, then we sing the octave from "do" to "do" followed by a major arpeggio. We repeat this over and over, climbing each time by half step intervals until we have reached the top of our range. Then we "climb down" by singing arpeggios, each one lower then the one before it, until we get low enough to add the second octave onto the first. (See appendix, Exercise 1.)

If you begin with a class as a formal singing lesson in grade three, not having had them previously, and the children are not used to it, at first they may be amused by singing so high. It induces a sort of vertigo to children who are unaccustomed to it. After a month or so, they will be quite used to exercising the full range of their voices, however, so do not pay too much attention to the giggles you will hear at the start. Not everyone's voice will expand to the highest notes right away. It is important to tell the children what to do if the notes get too high. They can simply open their mouths to sing, and if no sound comes out, that's fine. Caution them quite seriously against straining their throats or tensing up in any way. Demonstrate for them what it *looks like* when you do this, so they will relax their shoulders and throat. I say *looks like*, because I have had the rueful experience of singing in the wrong way for a class. The children had a dramatic demonstration of just how harmful it is, because I subsequently lost my voice for a few days afterward! Singing the high notes correctly can always be described by images; I use the image of a feather floating down from a bird's nest. Suddenly a puff of air gets under it, and it ascends, effortlessly and instantly. One's hands can illustrate this gesture as well. That is how the voice ascends, easily and lightly. If no sound comes out, that's fine. Once the children are relaxed, their ranges will grow upwards. Some boys in particular must constantly be encouraged to sing in the soprano range. Tell them about the famous boy choirs, and how they try to keep their highest notes for as long as possible. Some lucky fellows can even sing soprano as adults, as well as the low notes.

In some classes I have had, there are one or perhaps two boys who genuinely do not have a high range to their voices. At first I was convinced that the notes were in there somewhere, but I have been unable, even individually, to help them to find them. It may be with the increasing descent into materialism that some voices are just too heavy even during childhood (See the note on individual help for children in Appendix B). Let such children sing an octave below without comment or undue notice by his classmates. In the other direction, developing the lower tones, I would not carry these exercises below middle C until grade four or even five. There the children must be cautioned to watch for a warming of the throat, a warning of stress on the low notes. Children who feel this can stop singing immediately.

It would be good to give the music lessons a definite form. I begin with a verse. This is one I came upon by expedience when as a brand new teacher I was rushing across the school to my first music lesson with a fourth grade. "Oh," it came to me, "I should have a verse to start with!" Some good angel (new teachers, luckily, have this experience constantly) stepped in with one just as I entered the door, and I have used it ever since: I offer it below as a model only. The best verse is one you draw out of yourself:

> The birds do sing and so do we
> When we make music merrily.
> Our thanks to God, then we must give
> That with his music we may live.

Then we go right into scales and the other exercises that become an automatic part of every lesson. Once the scales are under way, there is one very good practice which is immensely helpful. Now that the children have the major and minor thirds, one can begin to name the intervals as they are sung. I use the image of a flight of stairs and refer to the game played by all children, jumping down from each step in turn, getting successively higher each time (Exercise 2). I draw the stairs on the board and give the intervals their names. Later in grade five one can introduce the "hidden" intervals, the minor fifth, sixth, and seventh, as a part of this exercise. My music classes have done this from grade three to grade five in every music lesson. Their intonation is excellent now that they are in the chorus, and I attribute it mainly to this exercise.

Exercises should be fun, and if they are introduced properly, the children will do them willingly. One would never run a race or swim a mile without first limbering up. This is our way of doing just that with our voices. Together we tune our instrument. Be inventive with exercises; there are hundreds of variations! Pitch and rhythm, and of course, practicing good tone production – all have their place in a music lesson, and I would not hesitate to spend fifteen minutes doing these before turning to the songs we are working on.

A first introduction to the staff and musical notation

In the second half of the year the class is introduced to the stave, the treble clef, which they enjoy learning how to draw ("Wow! How do you do that?" is often their reaction to seeing it drawn for the first time), and the pitch names. There are many ways to do this. Some teachers like to use the image of birds on a telephone wire, or to give each of the notes in their position on the stave a personality and a name. One could use the names of particular children in the class to identify the note positions. On the subject of teaching music, Steiner had this to say:

Of greatest importance, just in relation to our social life, will be the fostering of music in an elementary way through teaching the children straight out of the musical facts without any bemusing theory. The children should gain a clear idea of elementary music, of harmonies, melodies and so on through the application of elementary facts, through the analyzing by ear of the melodies and harmonies, so that with music we build up the whole artistic realm in the same way as we do the sculptural, pictorial realm where we similarly work up from the details. This will help to mitigate the amateurishness that plays such a part in music; mind you, it cannot be denied that musical dilettantism does serve a certain purpose in the social life of the community. Without it we should not progress particularly well. But it should be confined to the listeners. If this could be achieved, it would be possible for those who perform and produce music to find their proper recognition within our social order. For we should not forget that everything in the sculptural, pictorial realm works towards the individualizing of the human being, while all that is musical and poetical fosters our social life.... The individuality is supported more by the sculptural, pictorial element, and society more by the living and weaving in community through music and poetry.[15]

I think, taking this indication as a guide, it is possible to proceed directly to the notation without too many stories or laborious introductions. All along the teacher has been demonstrating the songs to the children by means of gestures for pitch, as well as by drawing the melodies on the board for them to see as melodic lines, on which the children can exercise their imagination to form into pictures if they are inclined to do so. If the children have already experienced the musical line through their pictures and drawing in earlier grades, they have an excellent perception of how a melody should look. To isolate the notes now as separate elements, I feel, is to violate the flow and unity of the melody. Therefore, I have the class sing an ascending scale. I remind them of the pictures they drew of melodies in the past. What would the scale look like? A mountain? Or just an ascending line? I then carefully draw a stave on the board, and show them a C scale written on the stave, explaining that a stave is like a frame, or clothesline, put there just to show which note is which. This gives a chance to explain the very special Middle C, the note that even has its very own line, one that only appears when C calls it into place! One can then proceed to some of the very simple tunes they remember from earlier years and put them on the board as well.

It is my personal observation that the presentation of the notes as separate pitches is best done with the recorder. In singing, it is the melody as a whole that can be experienced as it rises and falls across the musical line. One can, after all, sing a melody, even a written melody, on any pitch. It is the perception of the rising and falling of the intervals, the time signature and rhythm and, later, of the key signature that is helpful in learning to sight-sing. Once the staff and notation have been introduced, it can be used both in recorder lessons, at first for simple rhythm exercises focusing on one or two notes, and in singing lessons.

Rhythm exercises

In grade three, the rhythmic exercises are continued, of course, from the previous years. Note that they take on a purely musical aspect. Still using the words and images of the sun, rain-drops, etc., one can begin to construct rounds with these rhythms. The class still enjoys saying the words, but now we can begin to hold the words back, clapping or tapping where the words would go. Move slowly in this direction at first, and allow them to whisper the "lyrics." Two or three part rounds can be written very quickly on the board, just three or four bars worth for each part, in either three or four beats per bar. They can be made up on the spot in the classroom, for there is no harmony, and, therefore, no possibility of wrong notes! Over the course of the second half of the third grade, I begin to draw the pictures very quickly, almost using a "shorthand." It is no very great step from there to drawing the stems- the notation for the rhythms themselves, which can be done at the end of third grade. One can explain, for example, that the "rain-drops," because they are so little and quick, are like little children who must hold hands when falling from the clouds. See, there are their hands joined, just at the top of the stem. Sometimes only one appears alone. When that happens, you can see her little arm, just there, to remind us that she is part of a rain-drop. These rhythms are not written on the stave, but can be written, if you wish on a single line. Thus, the class can work on the rhythmic under-standing separately from the melodic placing of the notes on the staff. This is all brought together in the fourth grade when the class is comfortable with both.

Harmony in grade three

Many music teachers prefer to wait until grade four to introduce the singing of rounds to the class. Therefore, I have put the indications given by Steiner for harmony in the next section. You may wish to begin with rounds in the latter half of third grade, however; the easiest way to begin is with the teacher singing the sec-ond voice against the whole class; they are still singing in unison but have the experience of harmony. You may have eager singers who are quite secure musically who will want to sing with you on the second part. Many of the simpler melodies are suitable for this towards the end of third grade if a class is ready for it. If your aim is to challenge the class, rounds are the way to go. If your pri-mary aim is to give an experience of harmony, there is a better way. I have frequently taught the children a song to which I sing a second part once they are really secure. Thus, they get to hear the pure harmony of intertwining melodies without the jangle of words which happens in most rounds as the different parts of the same song sound together.

Fourth Grade

Now it becomes understandable that when a child first enters school, it comprehends melodies more readily than harmonies. Of course, one must not take this pedantically; pedantry must never play a role in the artistic. It goes without saying that one can introduce the child to all sorts of things. Just as the child should comprehend only fifths during the first years of school—at most also fourths, but not thirds; it begins to grasp thirds inwardly only from age nine onward— one can also say that the child easily understands the element of melody, but it begins to understand the element of harmony only when it reaches the age of nine or ten. Naturally, the child already understands the tone, but the actual element of harmony can be cultivated in the child only after the above age has been reached. The rhythmic element, on the other hand, assumes the greatest variety of forms. The child will comprehend a certain inner rhythm while it is still very young. Aside from this instinctively experienced rhythm, however, the child should not be troubled until after it is nine years old with the rhythm that is experienced, for example, in the elements of instrumental music. Only then should the child's attention be called to these things. In the sphere of music, too, the age levels can indicate what needs to be done. These age levels are approximately the same as those found elsewhere in Waldorf education.

Rudolf Steiner
*The Inner Nature of Music
and the Experience of Tone*

In fourth grade the children begin sight-reading in earnest, both in recorder and voice. I recommend that all advances in reading be made in the singing lessons, simply because our voices have so much more wisdom and mobility than our hands; there is not the additional complication of fingerings and position to deal with. If one is the singing teacher, this happens quite as a matter of course. (Class teachers can easily do the recorder with their classes, learning as they go along in order to stay ahead of the children, if necessary. If one is also the recorder teacher and must, therefore, combine singing and recorder, I would recommend dividing the teaching of notation between the recorder and voice sections of the lessons.) Taking Steiner's cue on teaching music in a matter-of-fact manner, I begin to introduce the basics of theory in fourth grade and carry it on through fifth. In my present school, the children go on to a chorus and different instrumental groupings in the junior high-school years. Grades four and five are the last chances to give the children, as separate classes, the basic elements of key and time signatures that they will be working with in the older grades. In other schools, where the class is kept together for instrumental practice longer, one could put off some of the elements I will mention until another year.

A note on scheduling

The following suggestion may be a headache for the colleague who makes up the over-all lesson plans, for it puts one more constraint on the master schedule. It has proven so valuable, though, that I recommend it highly. In the fourth and fifth grades, the classes can be arranged so that the singing teacher has one lesson each week with the fourth grade and the fifth grade alone. Another, third, lesson is scheduled (preferably at the end of the week, but not necessarily so) with the fourth and fifth grades together. This gives the teacher a large group to work with so that all the parts are strong. The children learn proper chorus decorum, the most important element being that they learn over the course of the year to listen quietly while the teacher works on one or another part. The fifth grade, for whom this is the second year as part of a Junior Chorus, can take the lower parts most easily, while the fourth grade, for whom this is all quite new, sings the easier soprano parts, worked on with the teacher during their weekly lesson alone. So much is gained from this that it is beneficial for the Upper Grade Chorus and the High School! Each week, the Junior Chorus begins the lesson in exactly the same way they always have: verse, then singing exercises. One can, of course, teach new material to the entire group, and as the year goes on, one should do so, but this enables the class to begin to sing in three parts early in the year, and more difficult, complicated music can be done more quickly. Meanwhile, the theory progresses at the appropriate pace in the individual classes.

New exercises for fourth grade

In grade four, all the exercises mentioned for grade three are continued, and the teacher should feel free to compose opening exercises. The children have been schooled to begin the music lessons this way, and they very much enjoy these exercises, frequently asking for particular favorites by name. I have put indications for a few new ones for this age at the back of the book.

The scale

We continue to sing scales and arpeggios at the start of each lesson, followed by the "half-step, whole-step" exercise. Teach them the minor scale and arpeggio, too. The class will find them very beautiful and will love to sing them. In grade four one can begin to ask the class to isolate these intervals and sing them separately from the scale, just as they have done with the individual elements of the times tables in math. I sing on a single tone the question, "Can you sing me a half step up from this tone?...Half_____ ." And the class joins in with me on the word "half", ascending a half-tone on the word "step," thus answering my question. Now take a different tone. "What about from here?... Half_____ ." Different again- "Half_____ ." As the class grows accustomed to this and gets better at it, I begin using whole steps and then minor thirds and major thirds. They need a bit of help, usually, in drawing the intervals out of themselves just at first, so we spend some time characterizing them.

Halloween time is a good season to talk about half steps. I use all kinds of images. "Have any of you ever stepped into a dark room, and you weren't sure where the furniture was?" I take a step while singing the first interval: "Half-step." "How about taking the first step down a dark cellar stair?" The class comes to see the tentative, minor quality of the half-tone by means of these visual, experiential images. The whole step is very different and should be presented at the same time for contrast: "How do you go out of your house on a beautiful day if you're going on a ride on your brand new bike?" Now have the class step forwards while singing "Whole-step!" The sunny, light filled quality of the major comes forward. Work on these intervals can take a class nearly through the first semester.

Later, similar images are useful with the minor and major thirds. All the children are aware of the cheerful, bright quality of the major third, but it can be quite difficult to isolate it from the scale. I use the arpeggio, and tell them to imagine the whole span of "do-mi-sol-do", and just sing the first two notes. The minor third is so different, however, and has the same tentative, darkened quality of the minor second (the half-step). One could try asking the class to stand up while singing the major third. They will do so in a sprightly way, drawn upright by the expansive quality of the interval itself. Now have them imagine that they wake up in the dark. The ceiling is a bit low, and they are not exactly sure how much space is above their heads. It will hurt if they bump it. If you have created a strong image, and then ask them to stand while singing a minor third, they will get it exactly right. One must constantly compare the major and minor intervals in order to be able to sing them independently.

Part singing

Of course, the class is eager to be able to sing in parts, like the older children in the school. For my classes I assemble a whole collection of music of all types; rounds, two and three part songs, music written in parts on one stave and on two and three, and also multiple-verse songs written in several ways – either with the words printed below the lines or at the end of the song. Most Christmas music is written two parts to a stave, like piano music. I include some of that too, as well as music with piano accompaniment, although I don't use a piano in my Junior Chorus. Throughout the entire year, we go through the various styles of scores, learning to find and follow the relevant parts, the verse numbers, the harmony, etc.

I approach written music much the same way as the reading was treated lower down in the grades. Everyone in the class may not always follow the notes or the text, or the dynamics just at first, but the important thing is to keep watching as we sing through the music. I actually tell them this, for your most melancholic child may well comment, "But I can't read music!" To which the only possible response is, "Not yet! Keep watching, though, and you soon will be able to!" This work with a text is quite separate from our work on interval recognition, tone production, and singing exercises. The children, of course, memorize the words and music very quickly, and are not inclined to keep their eyes on the page at first, so one begins to point out things about the music. At first, one must show them how to find their way about the page. Where is the title? Who has written this music? When? What about those words at the beginning – " allegro ma non troppo"? What is all this? With humor, a lively manner, and lots of pointing, we make our way in the first weeks. After a while, one can give the class a little test. "I am going to sing this song. I want you to listen and follow along, and when I stop, I want you to point to exactly that place in the music!"

Keeping time

Apart from the treble clef and the bass clef (which they will immediately ask about), the next thing to work through with the fourth grade is the time signature. Grade four learns fractions, of course, and they should readily understand 4/4 time, if you tell them that a quarter note ("sun" from last year) is worth one quarter of the bar. Four is the most natural time signature, since it is based on the physiology of our own being, so it is always best to begin with 4/4 time if introducing a new element in rhythm. Find some moment in the lessons this year to characterize the different time signatures as the dances they originally were. Show how 3/4 time moves in sweeping gestures as a waltz, 4/4 as a march, 2/2 as a clock or a heartbeat. Explain how 6/8 is a bit of 2/2 and 3/4 together. Once they are well on their way into their fourth grade math, they will follow with interest. Continue the rhythm exercises, now using the correct notation and give them individual copies to read from. They will at first find this difficult to do. The power of group learning is very strong – one of the challenges to any teacher is to help anchor what the class knows as firm knowledge in the individual child. This is true about every aspect of music as well. On the board, with all the children looking at the same exercise, every member of the class can do it, even if you call on them individually. Give each child a copy of his/her own to look at, and suddenly they are all at sea, even if it is something they have just done as a group successfully! (This always takes me by surprise.) Keep at it. Ask questions to make sure that you have all of them with you and be ready to spend time with those who don't get it to bring them along.

In fourth grade, once the class is quite comfortable with rhythm notation, eighth and sixteenth note rests can be introduced. Go back to the words, if you have already left them behind, and now the "rain-drop" becomes " * -drop", or "rain - * ". The sixteenth notes will be "Pit -* Patter", or "Pitter -*ter." Similar exercises in recorder on a single tone will establish this quite quickly. Speak the rhythms before playing them. In a song or a melody for recorders, it is important that the children grasp the fact that even though the notes may be floating up and down the staff, the rhythm is easy to read, and always follows the same rules. Be prepared for children to point out your mistakes when you make them! Find a way to characterize the dotted quarter note and its attendant eighth-note or rest. I sometimes use the image of a woman with a sore foot who walks with a cane along the road each morning. Demonstrate her pace, and emphasize the long step on the "good" leg. Her footprints in the road will be one firm step, with the imprint of the cane, followed by the light, small step of her sore foot! Later, of course, you will show the class the division on the bar into half beats (1-and 2-and 3-and 4-and). It is nicer if the children become acquainted with this rhythm in a more organic way first.

It is very good if the teacher knows how to conduct the different time signatures. Ask someone, if you don't know, and practice them while listening to music on your own. Learn what it means to conduct a 6/8 piece in two, for example, and be able to tell the class that you are doing this, and why. As you move through the year with your class, you will get better at it; hopefully you'll keep a bit ahead of your class. As a class teacher, you will need to be able to do this in any case when your class gets to playing four-part recorder pieces and the like.

Reading intervals in notation

One will begin to refer to the written music for more than just the words and the melodic line in singing. In your practice of the intervals in every lesson, for example, stop and show the class what a third, or a fourth looks like by drawing it on the board. Then, before turning to a song they are working on, ask them to find an example of that interval in the score (they can use the words of the text to identify it). Can they find a quarternote rest? What about a repeat sign? Explain dynamics, and have them follow the directions as they sing (the upper school chorus teachers will rise up and call you blessed). One soon runs into the fact that major and minor intervals look exactly the same in our notation. This is because our system of musical notation was "designed" for the scale of C. One can just ignore this until next year, or if you're bold enough and have inquisitive children in the class, you can plunge into theory. There is a way to do this, but it requires a long setting out, and you cannot spend too long on it in any one lesson. I tend to work at it bit by bit over the two years of fourth and fifth grades, in the separate lessons.

Perhaps before launching into the structure of the scale, the class might be interested in hearing how the music came to look the way it does. The earliest songs were taught by ear and by gesture, just as the children learned in the earlier grades. Then, in the Middle Ages, the hand gestures used were indicated, written over the words to the songs as little rising and falling lines, something like what they wrote in their books when they were younger. Then someone had the idea of showing the notes, just like the "stones" the pony stopped on to rest, and "hung" them on a rack of **four** lines, like little blocks, or diamonds. Give them a lovely bit of chant to sing, perhaps at Christmas, and decorate the page beautifully. Here again is a chance to isolate the melodic element in the music, for chant keeps its own time, just as one would say the words of the text. Now everybody the world over reads music in the modern way, on five lines just as they are learning to do.

Further steps in theory and notation

Have the children sing a beautiful major scale. Ask them to do it again and to listen carefully. Are all the "steps" they are taking the same size? A few will say right away that they are not. Now ask them to listen while you sing for them. "Raise your hand when you hear a smaller step." In my experience, at least half the class can hear the half-step intervals between mi-fa, and ti-do. Go back to the drawing of the steps one used at first to introduce the "step exercise." Now, show them that two of those steps are not as high as the others:

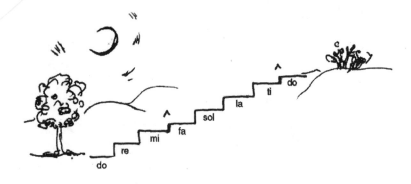

"What's the most important thing a carpenter has to remember and measure when he is building a staircase? What would happen if you tried to go up or down a staircase like this without looking?" Of course, we would all be flat on our noses at the bottom of the stairs. But our voices are much wiser than our feet. Our voice can go up and down this stair without ever faltering. Our voices are even cleverer than our fingers. Invite them to go home and play some song they know well on recorder, but start instead on a different note. The song will come out all wrong. But we can all sing that song, no matter what note we begin on!

Accidentals

Now write the scale on the board in notation and show them where the half-steps are. Those intervals look no different than any of the others, but our voices know the secret of the major scale. One can then show the pattern of the major scale: Whole step, Whole step, Whole step, Half, Whole, Whole, Whole, Half. I use this symbol above the stave: ^ to indicate the gap where the half steps are. In a few weeks, you might go through this again, as review, and take it further: "What happens when we sing a minor scale? What note changes?" Sing a major, and then a minor scale. The class knows by now that the third is flattened. But there is nowhere to write that new note! This is a good introduction to the flats and to the accidental, which they will certainly have seen by now in some music or other. E- flat must be written in the same space as E. The children like to learn the mechanism of accidentals and natural signs in the music. They will enjoy repeating the rules when you ask. There are always some in the class who easily remember that accidentals are canceled out at the bar line automatically. Of course, we must tell them that if we were writing a tune in which only the E-flat was used, we could just put it at the front of the music. Then all the E's would be flat automatically. Now one can ask a fourth grade to look at the sharps and flats at the start of their music as well.

Interval exercises

In the singing exercises, we can begin to work with creating harmonies out of their ability to sing the intervals. This can be done with the larger group of grades four and five, if necessary. Have one half of the class sing a whole step. Practice with the other half the singing of a whole step down. Now, starting on the same note, the entire class sings "Whole- Step" as they have just done. The result is harmony spanning two whole steps, or a major third. One can ask the class to identify this new interval sounding together. This can be done either by listening, or by working out the fact that one group has gone one step up in pitch while the others went one step down. What interval is two whole steps? This can be expanded, using different combinations of intervals. A major third in one group and a fifth in the other, gives a final harmony of a minor third. Why? The class will enjoy working this out.

We go through the year, sometimes sounding out new pieces by intervals, sometimes by ear with the class simply following the rise and fall of the melody in their music books. "Bona Nox" by Mozart is one they particularly love to sing. Since he wrote this for his sister when he was quite young, take the time to tell them something of Mozart. One can begin to introduce all the major composers, as well as their music, to the children in this way.

By the end of the year, I hope to have at least two thirds of the class sight-singing, at least in C, and able to understand the significance of sharps and flats in the key signature – not the complicated theory, but that they know these notes belong in the scale in which the piece was written, and that an accidental introduces a new note into the song. You repeat a lot, always gathering more and more children under your wing as the year goes on. The dreamy children will grasp very little of the theory you present, so it is important to balance your lesson; the in-breath of the more intellectual approach and the out-breath of the beautiful singing experience. Humorous songs and folk songs can provide some enjoyment and enthusiasm in the lesson if the children's interest begins to flag.

A caution for the music teacher

It has been my experience that music, when presented imaginatively and with a great deal of humor and love, is enjoyable and enlivening. But, occasionally — and this can happen at any level — when I have become too intellectual in my presentation, or have introduced something prematurely, the children let me know with their behavior. It is not necessarily that they become naughty, or inattentive, though that can happen, but that they – well, wilt is the best word for it. Several in the class may complain of stomachache or a headache, and while you may still have their good will, you will get nowhere with that particular approach. If you continue, the class will turn pale, and heads will go down on desks all around the room.[16] I have found it best when this happens to back away entirely rather than belabor the point, whatever it is, and let the children sing something they love and can do well. Thus, gently, one proceeds along the path of theory.

One can proceed with the theory further in grade four, if one has courage, an excellent understanding of music, and pays great attention to the signs the children will show you that you have gotten too far ahead of them. The more musical members in the class will certainly begin to ask quite complicated questions as the year progresses. Whether the answers are to be turned into a lesson for the whole class, or one just gives an answer to satisfy that child is a decision for the teacher every time. I have put the presentation of keys and key signatures in the section for grade five, where it is more easily taught, if it is to be taught at all.

Fifth Grade

In grade five, the singing program can be a continuation of fourth grade work, but on a more intensive level. If they have gone into a Junior Chorus, they should continue to have at least one music lesson on their own in which their reading skills are practiced and background knowledge of music in general is introduced whenever possible. The "theory" part of the lesson can be extended to occupy a greater part of the time occasionally. I stress that it is their responsibility to understand what I am teaching, and if they don't follow, they must tell me so and ask questions. I sometimes assign certain children the task of asking me a question the following week about something I have taught them. If they have not understood something and sit mutely, I will think they have grasped the concepts and will move on. It is necessary to actively encourage questions, for in a Waldorf school the pupils are not streamed, and one has children of all abilities in every class. This begins to show up in the music lesson when the material in the music lessons gets more complex.

Beauty in the musical experience

"In the tenth and eleventh centuries, [the] relation between external, materialistic music. . .and its heavenly prototype was still beautifully expressed. . . .People felt themselves transported to spiritual heights when they lifted themselves up from speech to music, which is the image of celestial music. This feeling was expressed in the following words:

Ut queant laxis
resonare fibris
Mira gestorum
Famuli tuorum
Solve polluti
Labii reatum
Sancte Johanne.

To translate this we would have to say: 'So that thy servants may sing with liberated vocal cords the wonders of thy works, pardon the sins of the lips which have become earthly...O Saint John.' Let us extract certain things that lie hidden in such a verse: Ut (this word was later replaced by do), resonare (re), mira (mi), famule (fa), solve (sol), labii (la), S.J. (si). ...The names of the notes in midieval musical notation, have been carefully hidden in this verse."[16]

As a counterbalance to the intellectual aspect of the lesson, one should remember to stress the beauty of singing. One should certainly refer to "Orpheus" in grade five! Perhaps the class teacher will permit you to tell the story in a music lesson. Keep nourishing them with pieces with beautiful harmonies. Use chime bars and invite other instruments as accompaniment occasionally. The exercises can get more complex as well. (Ex. 5, 6, and 7) A very beautiful musical exercise can be built on the early plainchant "Ut Queant Laxis." The children are very interested to learn that this song is the origin of our names for the notes in the scale. The song is beautiful in itself, but it can be worked on in the classroom in an exercise which my children called "building a cathedral." This could really be done at any time from fourth grade up to high school, depending upon the context in which it is put. The chant and the exercise are given at the end of the book (Ex. 8).

Some of the same choral pieces are used again in fifth grade. One can now teach the class the lower parts and ask them to begin to sight-read. It should be possible to put a simple to moderately difficult three part piece together in roughed-out form within a single lesson. These are the skills they will need next year in choir, if you have one. Those children, particularly, who think that music is not their thing, will need the challenges you present.

In the fifth grade one occasionally finds boys who, maturing a bit earlier than their peers (or just pretending to, which is worse!), have decided that they don't like singing. Adolescents retreat within themselves somewhat in the upper grades of the lower school, and boys retreat far more into themselves than girls do. In addition, they are all aware of the change in their voices that will be coming in the next few years, and some of them would like to wish away their lovely pure soprano in the rush towards adolescence. Lots of encouragement, humor, and a light touch are required here. An overbearing manner and a heavy handed discipline can turn such a child away from music forever. One must maintain a disciplined mood in the class, of course, but such children tend to make their feelings known one way or another. Just at this age, one begins to stress the lower alto range, or perhaps one actually has a few budding tenors already. By all means, find music for them that lets them exercise their voices! They will enjoy singing the low tones, and if they have become shy about their voices, one can always sing their part with them. Sometimes children become annoyed with the harmonious aspect of music - their souls are beginning to march to a different tune! Now is the time to bring in your guitar and tambourine. Regional folk tunes and amusing songs can lighten the mood enormously. (The class teacher should see to it that they are given access to the tenor and bass recorders as well.)

Developing skills in sight-singing

Fifth graders will come to understand written music more fully, so I show them how to find the do-note, which I call the "key" to reading the music. In addition to learning to sing the intervals and being able to recognize them in written music, I use the scale of the key signature in sight-singing in my classes, because I feel it is the approach which makes the melody most accessible to a singer. If one learns to understand the song with reference to the scale in which the melody is written, one will never need recourse to an instrument to be able to sing music on sight. (In instrumental music, playing the correct sharps and flats automatically places the notes in the proper relationship within the key.) It is also useful because one can then sing a given melody in any key. I frequently move a song up in pitch, for example, to make it more accessible to the budding baritones.

Beginning with a piece that is in the key of C, I have my classes sing the correct scale and then we "figure out" the song. I sometimes bring in music that even I have not yet sung or heard, and we learn it together: "Let's see. If C is do, does anyone know what note of the scale this song starts on? Yes, that's right. That first note, E, is mi." Someone notices that the next note is sol, then others in the class volunteer that fa, mi, re, and mi are the following notes. Now all we need is the pitch of the do-note. "Can anyone sing a C, do you think?" By fifth grade there are likely to be several in the class who are developing a good relationship to the absolute pitch values. Perhaps one or two have perfect pitch. This can be developed, and your careful exercises at the start of each lesson will go a long way towards assisting the children to recognize the pitch values in music.

Some weeks later, one might use the C scale, which one has put on the board as a review in class, to ask what would happen if we tried to sing a scale beginning on another note. Have the class sing the notes of the C major scale and ask them to continue on up to the high G . Now go back down, and stop at G above middle C. On a recorder, or someother instrument that is handy, play them the sequence of natural notes from G to G ' so they hear it in another timbre as well. The class will recognize, if you ask them, which note is "wrong." They should also be able to tell you that the ti (F') needs to be higher by a half-step. By erasing the first four notes in your scale in the key of C, and adding the notes at the top, showing the F#, the class sees how the G scale is written, and why the F# is needed. Check on the pattern now in place with the F# for Ti. It should be whole, whole, half, whole, whole, whole, half. "Yes, it is!" They will tell you. One can point out now in their music which songs are "in the key of G." G is the **key** to the song because it is "do!" Of course, they may already have learned the F# on their recorders, but now they know why it is needed in the songs they have learned.

I feel it is important that the children get a broad grasp of the reason why the key signatures are written the way they are. I feel, too, that it is good to do this in the singing lessons specifically. Ideally, they will also learn this in their instrument lessons. In learning to sight-sing, however, it is important to know the key and how to find your way about in the melody. This is a skill that takes years to learn, of course, and one must move very slowly, taking only five minutes or so in each lesson, but it begins in these years. After presenting the different key signatures, and showing the class how to find out which note is "do," one can begin to ask more detailed questions about the music at the start of a new piece. Where is "do"? What note of the scale does this song start on? Once a fifth grade child, impatient with some explanation I had embarked upon, asked me with, "What difference does it make what key it's in?" I pointed to the next song in our book. It was in D, clearly marked by the F# and C# at the start of the music and began with an eighth-note run from D' to A. "Can you sing me the first measure?" I asked. What a hard question! Was I being unfair? "Well, what if you knew that the first notes of the song were, "do, ti, la, sol? Does that make it any easier?" Ah! Of course!

The children thus learn the relationships of the notes of a melody to the do note. They enjoy being able to recognize whether a song will have a major or minor mood, by looking at the last note of the song. One can sing various examples of musical phrases, showing them how a cheerful song always "comes home" to do at the end. A minor melody frequently ends on "la." (This is actually the key note of the related minor scale, but this explanation is best left until the children are much older!)

Towards the end of the year, I give occasional tests to the class. I expect them to recognize individual notes, to place them correctly on the staff, and to understand time values and time signatures (to supply a missing eighth note in a 4/4 bar, for example). They should know the keys of C, F, B-flat, E-flat, G, D, and A, and how to locate do, and recognize the solfeggio name of any of the notes in those keys. I sometimes ask the children to write out a simple song that begins on do such as "Row, Row, Row your Boat"in notation, in a particular key.

From time to time, I remind the class of the fact that next year they will be in the Choir. These things will be expected of them! Work with the class so that they learn to read their music and look to you for direction and dynamics. Teach them how to hold their books so that they can do both. Make sure the children sit on the edges of their chairs, or stand with their weight balanced on both feet while singing. The more formal and demanding you make the requirements for proper singing now, the easier it will be for the teacher to handle the large combined classes in the older children's choruses.

Sixth through Eighth Grades

Chorus

The sixth grade is old enough to enter a more formal Choir, if one is available. In the schools in which I have taught, an Upper School Chorus is composed of sixth, seventh, and eighth grades. This is no longer the time for the study of music, but a class in which the practice of music occurs. The Chorus is large, composed of the entire classes and is a part of the daily schedule. When a well integrated music program has been established for a number of years, you may find that the class has risen to a level where a professional conductor, or at least a teacher with strong musical and choral training, is needed to keep the lessons moving at a good clip that engages your best musicians. The pace can be quite fast—the entering sixth grades are prepared for it each year, and are supported strongly by the seventh and eighth grades in the lessons until they find their feet.

It is a rare individual that can engage the attention of a large group of lively adolescents, keep adequate discipline, and maintain a mood conducive to good singing. Such people are treasures. Treat them like the exalted beings they are. I have always found that it requires at least two teachers to be scheduled for that lesson. That way the disciplinary measures (and they will certainly be needed from time to time) can be handled without breaking the flow of the lesson or of the music. An assistant must be available for organizing the music – a considerable task when everything needs to be in sets of seventy. A really good accompanist can be a huge support. S/he can lead sections from within the accompaniment when needed, and is sensitive enough to follow the conductor's wishes even when not specifically addressed to him or her. The chorus will need venues in which to perform. Festivals and outside engagements are vital to the perception in the children that this is a worthy activity. And lastly, the younger children must have opportunities to hear the chorus sing, so that they have something to look forward to.

To commiserate with and to encourage (if it is possible to do both of these things at once) any colleagues to begin such a Choir, I will recall the early days of a developing chorus program. It began in earnest nine years ago, when several teachers with a strong love of music appeared on the faculty of the school. The chorus class was somewhat rowdy at times, and it was difficult to control the kids who didn't particularly want to be there, as well as teach the music. One of the two teachers who took on the class needed to be the "disciplinarian," and the other conducted the chorus. They traded roles some years, since it is very demoralizing to a teacher to have to be a musical dragon all the time. There were some successful years and others in which the chorus seemed to be just treading water (forgive the misplaced metaphor – I might say they were holding a permanent fermata). There were children in the class who had no skills in reading music (having resisted the classroom instruction successfully) and were still not interested in learning them. Chorus was originally scheduled at the end of the day which, it was later discovered, the children thought of as an addition to their lessons! Since then, it has always been scheduled in the middle of the day, which helped to dispel this particular problem. For about six years the six, seventh, and eighth grade chorus performed an operetta each year to engender enthusiasm in the students for musical performance, and to encourage those who had the wish to sing solo parts to step forward and participate fully. These became quite successful and very popular with both students and parents. The children began to perform a cut-down version of Handel's *Messiah* each Christmas, both for the school festival and for the local community. All the while, the new sixth grades that entered the Chorus each year had a more complete understanding of notation and singing. The lower classes looked forward to the time when they would get to be in an operetta, and each year they heard the *Messiah* sung to a better standard. A few years ago the school reached the stage when chorus was either "cool," or else acceptable. Many openly enjoyed it. During the Advent season, one heard chance phrases and snatches of the *Messiah* arising spontaneously from the children as they went about their day.

Three years ago a prominent city conductor agreed to take over the Chorus. He enjoys working with the children very much and is able to draw on the willingness to work and the good intonation engendered by the children's experiences in the lower grades. The chorus can sight read and is very responsive. When asked to "round your lips to produce a good Ooooo," they do so without hesitation (with adolescents, this is truly a magnificent achievement, as anyone who works with them will tell you). When asked recently if there were any members who wished to try out for a solo part in Benjamin Britten's *Ceremony of Carols*, ten children stayed after class to inquire. This year, the chorus will sing at a Christmas service in the city's cathedral and will begin next year on the original, full version of Handel's *Messiah*, as their conductor is confident that they can do it.

When the class is asked to listen, on rare occasions, to recordings of other choruses singing some of the pieces they are learning, the children make comments like, "I like the way they sang that staccato passage at Rehearsal 25." Or, "I think we sing that part better than they did!" (The conductor agreed.) The baritone section is sometimes stronger than the altos! This last thrills me every time I hear them.

I insert this *Everyman's Tale* here as a reminder of the time it takes to build up a successful music program. I cannot imagine starting from scratch, for the skills and interest must be built into the children's expectations and experience and that of the parent body as well; this is a long process, extending over many years. Having built it into your music curriculum, however, and with the support of the faculty as a whole, you cannot fail to succeed. Begin now!

Music as science – the Chladni plate and the "shape" of tone

Although it goes beyond the scope of this book to discuss the main lesson curriculum, there is one subject that interfaces directly with the music teaching. The sixth grade studies physics, and one of the topics taken up in that period is acoustics. If I may be permitted to give non-class teachers a glimpse into the classroom, I will describe some of the demonstrations of this main lesson, as a beautiful example of the integration between the arts and intellectual study, a living interweaving of disciplines that breathes from the one sphere, in this case that of science, into the realm of music. Please do not use the examples given below as one's only source for a physics lesson, however. I am looking at the lesson from the point of view of the music teacher! There are many other aspects of sound that one may wish to emphasize in one's main lesson. For those who are not class teachers, I urge you to seek out a sixth grade teacher and beg them to show you the Chladni plate (available through AWSNA Publications) experiments; ask nicely and bring flowers and candy (whatever will work on a busy teacher's attention) —s/he may oblige you.

Physics is one of the first "hard" sciences the children come into contact with. The demonstrations of the physical properties of light, warmth, heat, and acoustics are objective phenomena to which the class brings its close and careful observation. The children are encouraged to remember and to write in detail about their observations in class, and the following day they are led by their teacher into a discussion of the principles they saw demonstrated the day before. Within the subject of acoustics, the teacher draws upon the musical experience of the class. It is here that the music teacher clearly supports the class teacher. Rudolf Steiner stressed that the "vocabulary" and experience of this section be a musical one.

In the first demonstrations, different things are struck with various objects. That blocks of wood produce sounds of different timbre than metal ones is apparent to us, but how many of us have actually listened to the sounding forth of the physical world? To do so is a musical experience. After many demonstrations of the qualities of sound involving timbre and intensity, the class comes to consider pitch. Musical instruments are used, mostly ones familiar to the class and in daily use; one compares the relative sizes of the recorder family, for example. After examples of many types of musical instruments, bottles, rubbed goblets tuned by pouring water into them, and the like, the monocord is brought out. This instrument has a single string, or at most two, and is used specifically to demonstrate proportion and measure in relationships of pitch. (A stringed musical instrument can also be used, but the only one with strings that are "stoppable" all the way up to the bridge that I can think of is a lute or a dulcimer.)

The teacher plucks the long, cello-like string. Then, carefully stopping it at the halfway point, the note is sounded again. "What is the interval?" An octave! Now the string is divided into thirds. After first plucking the whole length for the fundamental note, one third is stopped with a fret, and the remaining two-thirds of the string is plucked. "What is the interval you hear?" A class that has done its interval exercises for years will answer without hesitation. "A fifth!" If the initial pitch was, say, F, and one continues to divide the resulting two-thirds of the string into ever smaller thirds, always stooping the new length at the first third of the string, one will get the tones F, C, G, D, A, E, B. Place these pitches on a stave, and jump down the octaves (the last notes are very high!) so they are all contained within the staff. The result is the major scale, derived from the geometry and proportion of the vibrating string. The children may also recognize that this "Circle of Fifths" is the order in which the sharps appear in musical notation.

Now re-tune the string to a low B. One can divide the string by fourths, and pluck the string on the long side of the fret (the stopping point, at the ratio of $3/4$). "What interval is this?" A fourth, your class will/should answer! "The new note is an E." Now, using the new three-quarter length of the string, divide the string again by four and pluck three-quarters of it. Continuing to do so will yield the tones B, E, A, D, G, C, and F. The class will see that these are again the tones of the major scale, derived again from the mathematical division of the string. It is also the reverse of the progression that resulted the first time using the proportion of $2/3$. This is also the order in which the flats occur on the stave in their music.

The class has been able to recognize the intervals by using their own experience. They have seen the magic of the scale arising out of a single string. The physics lesson moves on through the following days. The children experience how the vibrating string moves, and see, by creating a standing wave on a jump rope, the "octave" nodal point — the place where the vibrating rope does not move, although it is oscillating on both sides of the center. The teacher can also demonstrate these "nodes" on the monochord, or on a guitar. It is at these points that the strings can be lightly touched after the strings are strummed without stopping the sound completely. Instead, a lovely, bell-like sound is produced.

At last one day the teacher stands by a strange flat metal object clamped to her desk. She holds an old cello bow in her hands. How interesting! With the class gathered around her, she asks someone to sprinkle sand, salt or, even more mysterious, lycopodium powder on the Chladni plate. She draws the bow across the edge of the metal, and the powder springs to life, moving across the plate into a clearly discernible pattern where the powder comes to rest. There is the nodal point, realized in two dimensions, on a plate instead of a string.

Touch the plate in the center of one edge lightly, and bow again. A higher pitch sounds, a harmonic of the first tone, and the powder leaps about once more, moving into a more complicated pattern. One can continue to do this five or six times, touching the edge lightly in different places and each time producing a different pattern, one for each harmonic tone of the plate. (These will not form a scale, or even be identifiable pitches, but depend upon the fundamental tone of the plate. The pitch of the fundamental tone is determined by the plate's weight, size, and thickness. The tones will all be related to each other as harmonic intervals, however. The class may be able to recognize the octave, and perhaps the fifth above it, but the pitches become too high after that.) These beautiful and varied forms and patterns arise magically at the incarnation of the tone into the plate that is bowed. It is one of the awe inspiring moments of the lower grades to call these unseen shapes into being before the children. Although one would not say such things to the children, here is what Steiner said about these figures:

> All kinds of figures will form depending upon the pitch of the tone. These are called chladni figures. ...Through the fact that the [celestial] tone sounded into the world of space, matter formed itself into a planetary system. You can see that the expression "celestial harmony" is thus more than an ingenious comparison. It is a reality.[21]

When as class teacher I have showed the children the chladni plate figures, I have paused to discuss the power of music the next day. Although one should not allude to the quote above, or discuss any sort of "occult" science in the classroom, they have all seen the patterns of a single sounding string, and those of a flat plate under the influence of musical tones. One should prompt them to wonder within themselves: What happens in three-dimensional space, in the room when we sing? What multitudinous, ever changing forms is the air conforming to, dancing invisibly around us in the hall, when we attend a concert?

Thus, one can hint at music's formative force beyond the physical effects touched upon in the physics lesson. This will also lead into a discussion of acoustics and sympathetic vibration, if that is wished.

Puberty and music

To any class teacher who has taught the upper grades, the above words may seem sometimes as if they cannot possibly go into the same sentence, unless one is talking about crashing cacophonies. Sixth grade is the time when boys in particular feel most vulnerable about their voices. The girls, too, sometimes need to take stock and retreat into their own inner spaces, for a great deal of change and development is beginning which is very private. The teacher must remember that our voices are always the revelation of our souls. Steiner speaks about our dealings as teachers with this tender age with some sensitivity:

> *Girls of this age will often acquire a kind of freedom of manner, they will be more ready to come forward in company; whereas in boys, and especially in boys of deep feeling, we shall notice more of an inclination to draw back. This will be due to the particular relation between ego and astral body that obtains in boys during the years of adolescence. . . .Withdrawal into themselves is especially characteristic of boys who have rather deeper natures; and the teacher (whether man or woman) can have a very good influence upon a boy of this kind by entering in a delicate manner into what I may call the secret that every such boy conceals in his soul. The teacher must beware of touching it ungently; but he can show by his whole demeanor that he is aware of its existence.* [21]

This is the time when some class teachers have given up singing in the morning, or, if they wish to continue, they must use every bit of creativity and imagination to keep the music going. It is a lot of work to get a class to sing with enthusiasm at eight o'clock in the morning! One can use good example, discipline, humor, and dire threats of detention: "We can sing now, or during lunch break. I don't mind which!" is probably a direct quote from the great majority of class teachers on one day or another in our careers. (Is there any class teacher who has never said this, I wonder?) It is very important that the music continue, however. This is the age at which they need every nuance of beauty and harmony the most. It was for just this journey into the rich and shadowy world of adolescence that you have been preparing them, musically speaking, all through their early years. None of us is too old or stale to remember the bursts of emotion, and the utter inability to express it that so delighted, tormented, and preoccupied us at this age. The astral body is coming to birth, and every parent and teacher within reach of this process is aware of its outward manifestations. But what is this body? Music is the vocabulary and the idiom of what has begun to pour through the floodgates of the soul.

True, the astral body expresses itself in the physical body, and this physical expression of it can be comprehended according to the laws of natural science. But the astral body itself in its true inner being and function cannot be grasped by these laws. It can only be comprehended by an understanding of music, not only an outward but an inner understanding such as could be found in the East and in a modified form was still present in Greek culture; in modern times it has disappeared altogether. Just as the etheric body works out of cosmic sculpture, so the astral body works out of cosmic music, cosmic melodies. The only thing that is earthly about the astral body is the time, the musical measure. Rhythm and melody come direct from the cosmos, and the astral body consists of rhythm and melody.[22]

After a discussion of the inner experiences and significance of the various intervals, Steiner continues:

This is the work of the astral body which is a musician in every human being, and imitates the music of the cosmos. And all this is again active in man and finds expression in the human form. If we can really come near to such a thought in striving to comprehend the world, it can be a stupendous experience for us.

How comforting it can be for a teenager to have the ability to pour these inarticulate birth pangs into a cello or a trumpet (depending upon temperament, of course!). To have been given the means by which to appreciate Mozart or Beethoven, or to take refuge for awhile in the ordered and even-tempered world of Bach is the gift of the music teacher to the developing individualities who sit or sprawl so awkwardly in their bodies and their seats at the moment.

Class teachers might find some of the ideas which have been outlined below useful for a general music curriculum of the junior high years.

Some diverging paths in curriculum

If a school has opted for a chorus in the upper grades, and also has continuing instrumental lessons, I have found that it is difficult to continue studying music within each class as well. In my experience, chorus needs to meet at least twice each week, and the instrumental teachers insist that good ensemble playing is not possible without meeting three times per week. As music teachers, we know that music is the single most important thing we can teach our children (I am convinced of this), but there are all those other special subject teachers who are clamoring for time with the students! Therefore, some accommodation must be made in the ideal music curriculum. Ideally, one would continue with at least one lesson each week for each grade, which could be a recorder, singing, or other instrumental lesson in which further theory would be elaborated. One could, for example, teach the minor scales and modes, cover musical biographies which follow the history and geography lessons, and develop skills such as conducting and even composition. Percussion, so often treated as an adjunct to music by the class teacher, and frequently handed to the least musical students to "give them something to do while we play recorder" (Don't! Give percussion to your best students, and let them experience the "harmony" of rhythm!), could be taken up as a special subject for a time. These, ideally, would be handled by the music teacher who has taken them all along, who would be able to integrate all these areas into a coherent music study.

If a school has branched out into several areas of music by the upper grades, the resulting diversification requires several different, and usually very busy, music teachers. They may be doing all, or some, or none of these things in their lessons with the students, and the chorus lesson is, as I have said, rightly given over to the making of music. Whichever above topics are covered, and they should be, they are incidental to the preparations for upcoming concerts and festivals. If class teachers were well prepared and enthusiastic, all of this could be incorporated into the various main lessons of the upper grades. I confess with some embarrassment, though, that I have not managed to include musical references in my main lessons as much as I should. It is my hope that if the teacher has an active musical life, this is carried into the classroom as a background to the lessons, whatever the subject.

Instrumental Lessons in the Lower School

...It is essential, for the inner processes of life between the change of teeth and puberty demand it, to give the children lessons in music right from the very beginning, and at first, as far as possible to accustom them to sing little songs quite empirically without any kind of theory: nothing more than simply singing little songs, but they must be well sung! Then you can use simple songs from which the children can gradually learn what melody, rhythm and beat are, and so on; but first you must accustom the children to sing little songs as a whole, and to play a little too as far as that is possible....As early as possible the children should come to feel what it means for their own musical being to flow over into the objective instrument, for which purpose the piano[24.]....is the worst possible thing for the child. Another kind of instrument should be chosen, and if possible one that can be blown upon. ...If you can, you should choose a wind instrument, as the children will learn most from this and will thereby gradually come to understand music. Admittedly, it can be a hair-raising experience when the children begin to blow, but on the other hand it is a wonderful thing in the child's life when this whole configuration of the air, which otherwise he encloses and holds within him along the nerve-fibres, can now be extended and guided. The human being feels how this whole organism is being enlarged. Processes which are otherwise only within the organism are carried over into the outside world. A similar thing happens when the child learns the violin, when the actual processes, the music that is within him, is directly carried over and he feels how the music in him passes over into the strings through his bow.

But remember, you should begin giving these Music and Singing lessons as early as possible.
Rudolf Steiner
The Kingdom of Childhood

In my experience recorder lessons in the lower grades usually fall to the class teacher. The following indications can be used by any teacher, but for those self-effacing "non-musical" Waldorf teachers, here is a wonderful opportunity to learn and grow with your children (or, preferably at least a bit ahead of them). It is possible to find yourself conducting a recorder ensemble in your classroom in seven years! The first steps are taken in grade one.

First Grade

The first advice I have to give as far as playing recorder goes is – **Wait!** Many of the children's hands are still too small and weak to effectively play recorder just at first. It is best if one puts it off until the children have grown a bit into their new life as first graders before embarking on the recorder. The children enter the first grade with tiny fingers that are not yet under their full control. In some cases, their fingertips are too small to cover the recorder holes adequately. All the dexterity exercises one does with them, from cutting out orange circles for their Halloween pumpkins to the finger knitting at which they work so enthusiastically, will help their progress in music, but there are a few particular things one can do with a first grade at the start of the year to help more specifically with their playing later on.

Preparation for recorders

Besides all the excellent finger exercises one can find in the many collections of Waldorf poems, and what can be gleaned from one's colleagues, to play recorder one has to be able to move each finger quite independently while the others remain quite still. It is good to use a rod, a small rhythm stick, or some such thing and have the children practice lifting each finger in turn while the others stay down. After the class has heard a description about a birds nest filled with babies, waiting for their mother to return with food for them, one has all the children hold their rods horizontally in front of them (that way the teacher can see the movement of their fingers clearly). As their fingers rise and return to their places one by one:

> In the nest upon the ledge,
> The little birds peep over the edge,
> One by one each moves and peeks
> While mother bird their breakfast seeks.

They must also develop skill in lifting several fingers in turn, and holding them up while others fingers move. Create the picture of the little birds in a row along the garden fence, and how they will learn to fly:

> Little birdies on a wall,
> One by one they fly in Fall.
> Summer comes and flowers spring,
> And all the birds return to sing.

One can create one's own verses for these exercises. The children will need lots of them, over and over each day. It will do no good, and will even frustrate the less dexterous children in the class, to hand out recorders before these finger skills are learned. One can use the same verses to emphasize the rhythm of the poems and see that the class can move their fingers as well as their feet to the rhythms.

The pentatonic recorder

In the meantime, one might begin working on the recorder pieces one will teach them once the children are ready. There are several good pentatonic songbooks, or one might create one's own songs. In either case, I recommend working with a Choroi pentatonic recorder well ahead of time to acquaint oneself with the gentle tone and mood of this instrument. This instrument is well suited to class work. (The pentatonic scale is one which has no half-step interval in it. See the discussion of songs appropriate to first grade in the Singing section for the reasons for using the pentatonic scale with young children.) Their whispering tone is soft, and overblowing does not give an octave or a shriek, but either no tone or a constant single tone, so the children are encouraged to blow correctly. The other advantage to using a pentatonic instrument, rather than simply teaching pentatonic melodies on a "normal" diatonic recorder, is that the holes which would produce the entire scale are not even cut into the instrument. The appearance is, therefore, less daunting to the child. Here is an instrument they can manage, that sings softly and sweetly. (Still in doubt? Just visit the third or fourth grade during their recorder playing and see that child in the corner with his hands over his ears during a particularly shrill passage.)

The first recorder lesson

When you judge the class is ready to meet the recorder, it is important to do everything possible to ensure that the children know how to treat a musical instrument with the respect it deserves. I have seen too many classes (thankfully not my own!) in which the boys alternately play their recorders and sight down the barrel to shoot down half their classmates during the half-note rests! The way a recorder should be held and used should be stressed right from the start in first grade. When introducing the recorder for the first time, a story could be told about a person who can make the trees sing as beautifully as the beautiful birds do. (Historical accuracy is not important here, but rather an imagination which will fill the class with reverence and love for the instrument). Here is a much abbreviated example:

One autumn day she walks through the forest when the leaves are off the trees, looking and listening for the trees that can remember the music of the summer and long so desperately to sing like the birds that have so lately departed to fly south. How will she find the right trees? There is no music in the forest now, but she knows well how to listen. She stands still as gusts of wind shake the trees. There two branches are rubbing together and squeaking. She smiles, and notes their places just there by the big grey rock. They will make good violin bows one day. But today she is looking for a different kind of wood. Ah! What is that sound? She listens again as the wind sighs through the branches. There! A little tree stands just there, holding its branches so that the wind hums through them as it passes. There is a singing tree! The woman rejoices, and the tree is happy too, because at last it has grown big enough to be noticed! The instrument maker cuts it down and takes it home. Slowly and with great care, while the winter snows fall outside, the wood from the little tree is fashioned into many long, thin tubes. Each one is stopped at one end, and carefully shaped inside to be smooth and round, like our lips are when we sing. Finally one day the little window that lets the music in, is carefully cut and shaped at one end. Then the instrument maker tries out each tube. In the little house the light warbling whistle of the new recorder sings like a bird. Finally, the tree can sound forth the music it has dreamed of making.

The recorders are given out, and the teacher instructs the class in its care. By now each child has already made a lovely soft case in which to keep it safe. The class can then be invited in a quiet, orderly way to come one by one to breathe upon a candle flame, making it dance and sway, but not go out, and then they try to breathe in just that way into their recorders. A song which they have learned that makes a rhythm on just one note would be a good first "tune" to play, but the teacher must have thought ahead and introduced it several weeks earlier so that the children know very well how it should sound.

The class proceeds over the next months from one-note tunes to two notes, and so on, until both hands are in place and all the holes can be covered. Progress is slow, and must be, for there will still be some little fingers in the class that need time to grow. Discipline is most important in a music lesson. The teacher must be ready to correct odd and deliberate noises in a friendly way and then, should that be unsuccessful, to remove the recorder of any child who plays out of turn. Be firm now. This is essential for your own sanity in years to come! Amusing stories about a girl or boy (not a specific child, of course) who cannot help but play out of turn and the consequences of that inability would help, but they would be better told outside the recorder lesson if possible.

Another way fingering skill can be developed is to teach the class how to play like the woodpecker might. If the instruments are held away from the mouth, the tapping of the fingers on the holes gives a little drum-like sound which yet has pitch. Songs can be "played" this way, too, which will strengthen the fingers, since the harder the fingers come down, the stronger the "note" sounds. The class is amused by this sort of recorder playing, and if everyone does it together, the sound is quite audible!

Second Grade

By second grade, the class can play, still by imitating the teacher's fingering, many of the songs they sing, and the time lapse between learning as melody, as a song, and as a recorder piece is not so important. The children can be called upon by row, or in small groups to show how well they can play, and there will certainly be individuals in the class who will occasionally (or constantly!) want to get up in front of the class to lead a particular song. Folk music, particularly Celtic tunes, are a good source of pentatonic melodies for second grade. By the end of the year one should be using all the notes on the instrument, teaching them in a matter of fact way as they arise in new songs over the course of the year. For the teacher, there are two ways to play the recorder: one is to show the children clearly what your fingers are doing. Instinctively the teacher exaggerates the motion as s/he fingers the notes. The other way is the way one should play the instrument, with the fingers held just a fraction of an inch above the open holes. Demonstrate to the class how it looks when you play the correct way, and play correctly when playing melodies that the class already knows. I try to remind the children from time to time all the way through the early grades that they should play the correct way, and that I am lifting my fingers so high in order to show them the notes clearly. Holding the fingers low over the holes makes rapid passages possible later on.

Pitch and rhythm – two exercises in developing musical skills

As the class moves along with technique, one can go back to the sort of two and three note melodies that were so hard in first grade and teach the class to respond as they do in singing, to the gestures of the teacher to indicate pitch. The teacher then "composes" tunes on the spot, using the entire class as an instrument as they respond to your gestures. Another very valuable listening exercise, which one could begin using such simple two note patterns is to turn your back to the class and play a simple unfamiliar phrase. They hear it, but cannot see how your fingers moved. Then ask the class to play it. Do this over the course of the year with increasingly complicated melodies. Thus, slowly, the internal experience of high and low notes which comes instinctively in singing is transferred to the external instrument of the recorder.

In the recorder class one could also use the game I described in the section on singing, of getting the children to recognize the melodies they know by indicating them either by clapping of the rhythm or by indicating the pitch of the notes in silence, using just the hand gestures of the melody. Once the class has become used to the positions of some of the notes, the teacher can hold the recorder out away from the mouth and finger the notes for the class to see, but not hear. The children who are aware right down to their fingertips will easily guess which song it is. Rhythms can be worked with as well on recorder as in singing, using the pictures described earlier in the book for the quarter, eighth, sixteenth notes, and triplets: Sun, rain-drop, pitter-patter, and buttercup in single note patterns.

Structure of the lesson

If the teacher is able to schedule a whole period for music in the first or second grade, some of that time should be spent telling stories, which emphasize the magical qualities of music, which are about the recorder, or which give a full introduction in story form to the songs the children will learn. It would be difficult to spend a whole lesson playing music in first or second grade, for the music has an excarnating, exhilarating effect on young children, and one will have a host of wriggling, squirmy bodies on one's hands unless the class is led to some more inward activity like drawing or listening to a story.

Third Grade

Introducing the diatonic recorder

In grade three the class's lovely soft Choroi recorders are retired, and the diatonic recorder is introduced, as are the stringed instruments. Many schools prefer to wait till a good part of the year is under way before putting a "normal" recorder into the children's hands, but I think there is something to be said for starting the year with the new instrument, and transferring several of the simpler songs they already know on their old Choroi recorders to the new fingering. Either way, the teacher will find that the discipline instilled in the music lessons in the earlier grades will begin to show now. A carefully thought out introduction before the instruments are brought out in the lesson is advised, and it is good to have consequences in mind before the lesson if one has any of those mischievous fellows who will want to put the new recorder through its paces right away. Giving these recorders to children, as Steiner himself said, can be quite a hair-raising experience. Even the children who are making the worst noise will complain that the sound makes their ears hurt! And those sensitive souls in your class will certainly not find it a pleasant experience. Again, one has to instruct them in how to blow, for now overblowing will produce the octave. Again, fingering has to be taught, one note at a time. The diatonic recorder has the additional complication of "cross-fingering"; in going up the scale, one sometimes has to replace one or two fingers lower down on the recorder to produce a tone which is in tune.

Scales and exercises

The C major scale is taught almost at once, and we use it as an exercise in fingering at the start of every lesson. I have always taught the D major scale early on in the year as well. The class has still not been exposed to written music and its absence means that the teacher has free range over all the keys, and can teach the fingering of any sharp or flat required by a melody. There is no need to explain that a C and a C# are related; one simply plays them each in their context within a piece, or in their different scales. By the end of the year, the class will have mastered the C scale and the D scale, is perhaps learning the F major scale, and can play several of the simple rounds they had learned as songs in the second grade. I give the class several fingering exercises to work on, a little each day. (See Recorders, ex. 9 and 10.) It is good to begin to identify the initial notes of the songs one introduces. "This new song starts on G. Gerry, can you remember which note is G?" Thus, the pitch names can be learned throughout the year. The class might like it if the notes are given "proper" names – perhaps the names of particular children (Albert, Beth, Carly, David, etc.) in the class, to aid in remembering which note is which, but beware of trivializing the musical experience with too many cute names. I have found it easiest to give the children a "home" note as the first one to connect with a pitch name, and on the soprano recorder I use G, simply because it is the easiest to play. When one picks up the recorder in one hand to begin, the fingers fall naturally into that position.

The stringed instruments
The lyre
In third grade the children get their first experience of a stringed instrument. One might say that we are moving the experience of music out of the physical body and into the surrounding space. The child's first musical experience is with singing, then the recorder, an extension of the breath. At the start of the third grade they hold in their hands a lyre or a cantela, small harp-like instruments with ten or fifteen strings. The instrument is embraced with both arms, and the tone is soft and sweet. Again, simple songs are taught through imitation, only now the tones are laid out before them, and the children get the experience, in a different way, of the placement of a melody. One can use chime bars and other instruments within the class to accompany their music and give back to the children some of the beautiful, embracing quality of music that will fill them with contentment. (This quality is now absent from their recorder lessons, which are more bright and hard in quality.) This stage of musical experience might be lengthened to last for the entire year, thus putting violin at the start of grade four, if desired, but I certainly would not shorten it or leave it out. The children have heard the story of the Fall in the main lesson – they have been told that the earth is a place for work, and while they certainly embrace the work with enthusiasm and love, here is a chance for them to experience some of the memories of heaven of which Steiner speaks when discussing the deeper aspects of music. The lyre lessons are magical.

The violin
Sometime after Christmas, one day the third grade children see new instrument cases on their desks at the start of the instrumental lesson! Their teacher stands

before them and introduces the class to this new instrument, perhaps telling them how s/he first met it as a child, or some story which will engender enthusiasm and love for the instrument. Then they are told they may open the cases and look at the violin where it lies nestled so beautifully within the case. They look while the teacher tells them how fragile it is and asks them to look at the delicate bridge where it lifts the strings high over the instrument's belly. When they are allowed to lift it out of the case, they look at its back and examine the slender neck. Then the instrument goes back into the case, and the class begins to make the acquaintance of its parts as the teacher demonstrates on his own instrument. Perhaps the teacher ends the lesson by playing a tune for them.

Over the succeeding weeks, the class is taught how to pick it up and hold it under the arm for carrying. They are taught about the bow in a similar manner, and hear about how bows are made of horses' tails. They practice stretching out their arms and holding the instrument under their chins, close to their own throats, and are allowed to pluck a tune upon the open strings. Progress is very slow, but the teacher can enliven it by having the class memorize some simple open tunes and pluck them while the teacher accompanies them with a beautiful, soaring descant. (It is important that the teacher inspire the students by beautiful playing.) At last the class is bowing the open strings. All the while, the discipline is gently, but firmly held by the teacher. By the time the first fingerings are taught, the class has learned the correct posture, demeanor, and attitude towards the instrument. This is of vital importance for your future strings program!

Again, the same rhythm exercises can be done on the violin as on the other instruments and in singing.

Fourth Grade

Then come the Fourth, Fifth, and Sixth Classes. By this time you will have got on well with explanations of the signs and the notes and will be able to make comprehensive exercises with scales....But all that is really essential is this: that you begin to work in the opposite direction. The child's attention will be directed to the claims of music, therefore the lesson will be directed more towards the aesthetic aspect. . . .When the child has passed through the first three classes where he himself was the first consideration, he must conform to the demands of music as an art.

That is the main consideration from the educational point of view.[25]

Rudolf Steiner
Three Lectures for Teachers

Notation in earnest

To gain a clear idea of how one might proceed with notation, please read the section for singing in grade four along with the specifically instrumental indications given here, for I feel that most of the advances made in reading music are most easily made in the singing lessons, where the "technique" that must also be learned as we go along is more instinctive and natural.

This is the year of notation! The class is learning the rudiments of it in their singing class, and hopefully, all the music teachers (and the class teacher) are working together to establish some common terms. The children will accept it if you are calling eighth notes "rain-drop" and their strings teacher calls them "blu-u", but it is more aesthetically pleasing for them and for you, if the musical teaching is consistent. This "musical Babel" will not last too long in any case. At some point during the fourth and fifth grades, you will all be calling eighth notes by their right names. In recorder class, the children are shown a musical staff. The lines and spaces are given their names, and the class can perhaps be given the opportunity to make up their own sentence for the order of the letters. (Every Good Boy Does Fine is appalling in a grammatical sense, but I'm afraid I'm stuck with it. At least I can invite my classes to come up with something better!)

Here one can be creative if one wishes. I have seen one teacher's beautiful illustration of a monk who had been trying to find a way to make a picture of a melody and was suddenly struck by the way the shadows of the leafy branches of the tree outside his window fell across his paper one moonlit night. Perhaps a nightjar flitted through the branches and gave him the idea of the notes moving across the lines. The names of the notes were the names of his brothers in the monastery. This made a beautiful picture for their music books. I feel, however, that sometimes Waldorf teachers are guilty of too much "window dressing." One should not use stories for everything! There is no harm in simply presenting the lines and spaces, and giving the image of a "rack" on which the notes are put, just so that we can see which note is meant. They will already be familiar with the single line for percussion notation, if you have started the year with the transition of the pictures for "sun" and "rain-drop," etc., into musical notation (see singing, grade four). They can easily grasp that if there is more than the single note of percussion, there must be more than one place to write it. The system of musical notation is very arbitrary, after all. There is nothing "true" about it except that it is our experience that a high note is, in fact, high. Rudolf Steiner recommended "teaching the children straight out of the musical facts without any bemusing theory. The children should gain a clear idea of elementary music. . . .This will help mitigate the amateurishness that plays such a part in music." I have introduced the "elements" of notation without stories, and I have not found that the children are confused or lost in the experience, but appreciate the clarity. A class can proceed with notation quite quickly, particularly if most of the musical vocabulary has already been given in the singing lessons.

With reading music, remember that one is introducing quite a complicated system to the class, and one should be aware of the different aspects of it. These simple five lines carry a lot of information! The range of the notes in the particular piece (the treble or bass clef), including the key in which it is to be played, the underlying beat of the music, its particular rhythm, the pitch of each note, as well as an indication of the general flow of the melody, how long each note is held, how to play it (stressed, staccato, legato) and the varying dynamics (p, pp, mf, fff, as well as cresc. and dim. and the like) of the piece as a whole with all the indications for the composer's intentions, as well as the mood and relative speed at which to play it — whew! There's a lot to look at! It's important not to complicate things any further for the children by trying to do too many things at once. The teacher should clearly focus the class's attention on one aspect of music at a time. Rhythm can and should be worked on separately from note identification.

First exercises in reading for the recorder

This is quite a different skill than it is in singing. Our voices sing quite unconsciously. We inwardly hear a note or a tune, and we simply sing it, without being aware of what our vocal cords have to do to make the adjustment between one tone and another. We don't even think of it. We just sing. With instrumental playing, one is building connections between a visual signal – the notes on the page – with one's fingers. The conscious will has (hopefully) mastered the fingers by fourth grade – all the education of the child up to now has been directed to just that aim among others. Drilling the notes is necessary and important to make the connection between the A on the staff with the position of the fingers on the recorder. It must eventually become as unconscious as the voice.

I begin reading exercises by writing the C major scale on the board. The class plays the notes while I point to them one by one. After they are comfortable with that, I warn them that I will try to trick them! Now I go up and down the notes, repeating some, and backtracking from time to time, just one note up and one down at first. The G is easy to remember, so I start from G and "play" a tune by pointing to the notes. This, done every day for a few weeks, will enable the class to play a simple melody that you have written on a large piece of paper that you can take down and put it up again the next morning. Many in the class will be playing by ear, of course, and not reading the music at all. Keep working at it. More and more of the children will get the idea as the year progresses. Do not be surprised later on when you give them their own copy of a piece of music for the first time. They will not be able to read it! They work as a group when they are looking at the same thing together on the board. As individuals many will be quite lost at first in reading. It is best if the first "sheet" music they are given is something they have read many times from the board, and it helps if the teacher goes over it again, pointing out the treble clef, the notes, the rhythm, and the like as if they have never seen it before. (Some never have seen it before, for they weren't looking in a conscious way at the board in the first place!)

Have the children read the music in small groups fairly early on. By letting the weaker children feel that they can be lost in the crowd, they will not be encouraged to put forth the effort required to read. There may be those in the group for whom the notation just doesn't make sense. Dyslexia, attention deficit, and a host of other identifiable learning differences make musical notation extremely difficult for some. You will carry these children for many years in the class. I am now giving recorder lessons again to some students in seventh grade, who didn't get it the first time round. I am pleased that they still retain an interest and a desire to master this skill.

Don't hesitate to move into two part music fairly quickly. The second part can be quite simple – just one or two notes throughout, which you can give to those who are not moving as quickly as the others in the class. In addition, it is possible to include the notation for a percussion part if one has a large class. They should well be able to play some quite fast pieces by ear, even if they don't yet have the skill to read them. Fiddle tunes are especially good at this age, and the class will enjoy the challenge of going as fast as they can!

Eventually you will be giving them sheets of music. Key signatures should be explained as simply as possible: "That means that all the F's in this piece are to be F sharps. Does everybody remember how to play F sharp?" Be prepared with simple answers to the questions about anything that is written on the music you eventually will be giving them throughout the year. I would leave the ideas behind key signatures to the singing lessons where, I believe, such things can be dealt with more easily. (See grade five, developing skills in sight-singing.)

A note for the class teacher: Begin to learn the fingering for the alto recorder now!

Violin

In violin, the class proceeds as it has in recorder. The class has been playing in unison, and towards the middle of the year, they should begin with some simple harmonies and two part pieces. The class works its way over the course of the year from imitation and playing by ear towards reading simple pieces in notation, perhaps going through an intermediate stage of learning the notes as an association of string and fingering (e.g. 4th string, third finger). The Suzuki Method is particularly compatible with the way music is taught in other classes, and the violin teacher should adapt what is appropriate from that system. Towards the end of fourth grade, a simple method book could be used in class for violin teaching.

Fifth Grade

The family of recorders

In grade five, many Waldorf schools introduce the rest of the family of recorders, at least the alto and tenor (only a few fifth graders will have hands that are large enough for the bass recorder). This can be done in a variety of ways. The new and quite beautiful sound of the alto engenders fresh enthusiasm in the class, and one can use it to sweep up the stragglers who have remained behind in reading skills to give them a fresh start – they haven't learned the soprano fingering anyway and, therefore, will not be confused by the change, and they are now a year older. Separate lessons will probably have to be made available to the new alto players, however, outside of class time. Another option, the one I prefer, is to give the alto to your best players, for they are the ones who will learn it most quickly, while the others continue to practise their soprano fingering. Yet another way is to teach the entire class the alto recorder in grade five, and then some of the able ones can easily go back to the soprano fingering and pick up the tenor recorder as well.

The tenor is a good recorder for those with larger hands who have already become adept at reading – the only thing they have to do is to get used to a larger span, for the fingering is the same as the soprano they already know. The class teacher must choose an option that best suits the particular class. This leaves aside the bass recorder, which has the alto fingering, but also the additional complication of being written in the bass clef. This, I fear, requires yet another special lesson time. It will seem as if your lovely recorder skills have disappeared for awhile, while all of this adjustment is going on. Courage! All is not lost.

Once the class has gained proficiency with these different recorders, the question of repertoire must arise. The class must continue to practice reading skills, but the job of supplying them with material has suddenly gotten much more complex. A good recorder book will come to the rescue now. Many of your colleagues will probably have hidden caches of sheet music at home. Ask them!

One can feel rather at a loss during the fifth and sixth grades in one's search for appropriate recorder music. The temptation will be to go to the beautiful Renaissance music too early – there is lots of it about, and all written for quartets and trios – but only the simplest pieces will be appropriate. It is often quite ornate and does not really suit the age of the children. The history curriculum is no guide during these years as it is in the upper grades. There is no record of what ancient music sounded like, although we know what instruments they played, nor is there any trace of Greek or Roman music. Plainsong for the sixth grade can only be done so much.

I feel that it is best to stick with early music or folk music. Look, for example, for arrangements of regional or national folk songs which will complement the geography curriculum. This music is simple in harmony and style. One can certainly introduce Mozart and Bach, any easy "classics" to the children. They can also learn to play many of the tunes they have sung in choir. At this age you are bound to have some children who are learning instruments privately. Don't hesitate to invite them to play their own instruments in class and start an "orchestra" that could practice for twenty minutes in the morning twice a week. Percussion of all types adds a sparkle to simple recorder pieces. The music lessons across the board continue to develop skills in their various techniques, and all should be emphasizing reading skill, particularly the more complicated rhythms. Syncopation can be introduced in its simpler forms as clapping rhythms (1 **and** 2 **and** 3 and 1 **and** 2 **and** 3 and). The class should move away from the picture words for rhythms, except where necessary to make sense of a difficult measure.

Continue working with scales during recorder practice as warm-up exercises. This is a little more complex now, for there are two sets of ranges and fingerings in the class, but they do share some scales. F, G, and A can easily be played in their different octaves, for example, and the sopranos will need to learn the fingerings for the notes above the staff anyway. Write out these scales, and play and point as you did in grade four to accustom the children to reading above the staff. Here is where your private recorder practice of the previous year will shine. If their teacher can switch easily from one recorder to the other, the class will be deeply impressed.

Strings

In my present school, this is the year in which the class also meets a division in the violin family. The teacher chooses the students who will play viola and cello, and here method books really are useful, for the same piece is written out in the different clefs in their books. I feel that during the course of this year the children should learn to tune their own instruments, although a teacher with sensitive ears will certainly suffer at first, and supervision during tuning may require the presence of another teacher in the class to prevent damage to the strings or bridges.

Providing new instruments, expenses, and storage

As children grow older, the expenses of the school and to the individual families grow as well. The expansion of the class into different recorders and strings requires either an additional outlay from the parents or an investment on the part of the school to supply the instruments. One can simply ask the parents to provide them. Many are quite able to do so and are certainly willing. In my present school, we have come up with a system that is workable and fairly inexpensive. I offer it here for what it is worth:

One year the school put aside extra funds in the music budget and purchased five or six alto and tenor recorders and several basses. These instruments were rented to the families of the fifth grade for an annual rate that was about one third the cost of the recorders. This rental money was used to purchase several more recorders which were saved for the upcoming fifth grade the following year. The next year, the same recorders were rented again to the (now) sixth grade, and the funds from the new rentals were put to purchasing additional recorders for the new fifth grade, which were then rented along with the ones that were previously purchased (from the rental money from the year just passed).

Since there are always a few families who are in a position to purchase their child's recorder as well, in two years the school managed to provide a renewable music budget, and enough instruments for the classes to use for only the initial investment that first year. It is actually possible to give the recorders to the children if they are going on to high school after the third year of rental, for the funds have become self-renewing after three years and there is enough money to supply the new fifth grade each year with recorders.

Each school must plan how to provide the violins to the children. In many schools the parents provide them willingly as a part of their obligation. Then, at the end of each year a "swap meet" is held to find a larger instrument, sell the old violin that has become too small, and the like. In some areas where tuition is high and incomes are low, the school might be reluctant to put the extra burden of expense onto the parents' shoulders. Then the school must fund-raise for the purchase of an adequate number of violins, violas, and cellos to give a jump-start to the strings program. The instruments are then rented out, much as the recorders are in the section described above, with an additional "string fee" for the year. The income generated from the rentals can become a starter fund for the purchase of still more instruments, as well as a source for much needed repair money.

In planning your music expenses, do not neglect proper storage, which is essential and will save a good deal of money, time, and hassle in the long run.

In addition, other funds are needed, of course, for capital outlays in the music department, for stands, sheet music, and the like. It is the music "person" who must make sure that the line for music is not forgotten in the annual budget!

The Upper Grades

And in the last two years, the Seventh and Eighth Grades, I ask you to note that the child should no longer feel "drilled," but should already have the feeling that he studies music because it gives him pleasure, because he likes to enjoy it as an end in itself. It is towards this that the so-called music lesson should work; thus in these two years musical appreciation can be formed.

The particular nature of different musical works of art can be brought out; thus the character of a piece by Beethoven or of Brahms can be brought to the fore. Through simple forms the child should be brought to exercise musical judgment. Before this, all musical discrimination should be kept back, but now it may be fostered. [26]

Rudolf Steiner
Practical Advice to Teachers

Grades Six, Seven, and Eight

I have chosen to lump these grades together because as one goes up the grades, it becomes clear that the teaching of music proceeds at its own pace. All the basic concepts have been introduced. What remains is to use them as often as possible! If one still has one's own class for a separate music lesson at these ages, one continues to work at all the aforementioned aspects of music, particularly in grade six, until the class is quite proficient.

The instrumental music lessons – a suggestion for scheduling

In my present school we have adopted a course for some years now which has worked very well. The entire sixth, seventh, and eighth grades are carried along in our instrumental program, as they are in our chorus. During the periods set aside for instrumental playing, this large group divides into three sections (this number is arbitrary and is based upon the teachers with necessary expertise who are available to lead the sections).

One group goes to the String Ensemble. This is usually a select group of children who, after all, have been studying the violin in the school since third grade and includes those who are doing well on the newer instruments of viola and cello. In addition, those children who show promise, but have not quite become proficient enough are allowed into this group provided they are engaged in private study with a teacher (preferably our own strings teacher – this gives some continuity in the scheduled music lesson, and incidentally helps to fill out the teacher's time-table and provide the extra income that makes it profitable enough for her to teach at our school).

The second group is a guitar/ukulele group. They work on repertoire appropriate to their instruments. This group often includes children who have joined our school in the middle grades and have not had the background in violin from which their classmates have benefitted. They are new to music in general, frequently, and are just learning the rudiments of recorder in a special afternoon class.

The third section is a Band Class. These students have worked at violin for years and have shown in manifold ways (ask the strings teacher to elaborate on this, if necessary!) that the violin is definitely not their instrument. Using mostly rented instruments, these children start again in sixth grade to learn a new instrument, brass or woodwind, and since the reading of music is not entirely new to them, they generally make quite good progress. Some guidance in selecting which instrument to play is needed, which takes both the temperament of the child and the configuration of the ensemble into consideration. (One year I had seven saxophones in my group!) The class uses a method book for Band and practices in the most sound-proof room in the school. Hopefully, the teacher of this class has a good sense of humor and a knowledge of transposition or, better still, is actually a band teacher! Through this class, we are able to supply our high school orchestra with brass and woodwind players who have the requisite musical skills.

One could, if desired, also schedule a recorder class during this period, either for those who have a genuine love of the repertoire, or for those who have joined the school late in the process and need to learn basic music skills to be able to participate in their class recorder playing.

Recorder in the separate classes

In these grades, recorder should continue for the entire class most mornings in the main lesson, even if for only fifteen minutes or so, as does singing. The Waldorf curriculum for history is quite specific, beginning with the span from ancient Greece to the Middle Ages in the sixth grade, the Renaissance in seventh, and the Age of Reason right up to modern times in the eighth grade. In addition, the scope of geography widens tremendously, so there is ample material from which to draw the music for these morning activities. Henry VIII's "Pastime with Good Company" is a particular favorite with the seventh and eighth grades. The class now can play, and frequently sight-read, Renaissance and Baroque music in four parts, and the class teacher should now feel competent enough to direct. The chorus can sing pieces like Britten's "The Ceremony of Carols," and the like. In the string enemble, perhaps the children are working on Pachelbel's *Canon*. If all has gone well, music has become a pleasure, and as it did in the early years, it unites the class each morning in a common experience of beauty and harmony which is deeply satisfying. It does more, too, for the children have been provided with a musical foundation, a vocabulary of the soul, if you will, for their entire lives and even beyond, into the world after death.

If you let this thought ripen within you and bring the requisite enthusiasm to bear, conscious that by developing an appreciation for speech and music precisely during the grade-school period, then you are preparing that which man carries with him even beyond death. To this we contribute essentially with everything we teach the child of music and speech during the grade-school period. And that gives us a certain enthusiasm, because we know that thereby we are working for the future. In that which reaches into the future we infuse our own forces, and we know that we are fructifying the germ of music-speech with something that will operate into the future after the physical has been cast off. Music itself is a reflection of what is of the (celestial) spheres, in the air - only thus does it become physical. The air is in a sense the medium that makes the tones physical, just as it is the air in the larynx that renders speech physical; while that which is nonphysical in the speech-air and is nonphysical in the music-air unfolds its true activity only after death. That gives us a certain enthusiasm for our teaching, because we know that when working with music and speech we are working into the future.

So that you understand the matter still better, I should like to mention that music has its being principally in the human astral body. After death man still carries his astral body for a time, and as long as he does so, until he lays it aside completely. . .there still exists in man after death a sort of memory; it is only a sort of memory of earthly music. Thus it comes about that whatever in life we receive of music continues to act like a memory of music after death, until about the time the astral body is laid aside. Then the earthly music is transformed in the life after death into the "music of the spheres," and it remains as such until some time prior to the new birth. . . .

The matter will be more comprehensible for you if you know that what man here on earth receives in the way of music plays a very important role in the shaping of his soul-organism after death. That organism is molded there during this period. . . .We furnish the possibility that the human being will be better formed in his next life if during that time after death, when he still has his astral body, he can have many memories of things musical.[28]

Appendix A

Private Study for Students

Voice lessons

Occasionally one meets a child whose musical inclinations have prompted a wish in the parents (or, occasionally in the child) that the child excel in musical performance at an early age. I have been approached by kindergarten parents twice, asking if I could recommend a voice teacher! The answer is a most emphatic "No!" Children's voice training, if such a field could be said to exist, is a dangerous area. The qualifications given in this book for adult students when considering vocal training must be even more heavily stressed for children. Their voices are still almost archetypal, and singing should be almost unconscious. One does not want a young child to be focusing on how they sing. A too early training will encourage them to "insert" a false personality into their voices, and the result is often obnoxious, giving them the sort of showy quality that one associates with cute top hats and sequined dresses. It focuses the child's attention on "producing" the voice and projection, when what they should be experiencing at a young age is the ethereal beauty of a sound that still should seem to come from the cosmos, not from them at all. By all means discourage children younger than grade six or so (when the astrality is at least there to work with) from studying voice!

That said, there are frequently things one can do to help a child who has been asked by his/her teacher to sing a solo in the class play in the upper grades. Frequently children "mask" their voices by putting too much breath into their tone. This makes for a very sweet, whispery tone, the kind deliberately used by blues singers, for example, but in a child it makes the voice very difficult to hear. I have worked with such children – girls usually, since they are quite willing to come forward to sing in such situations – to get them to place the tone they are singing "on top" of the breath, rather than to wrap it up in a blanket of air like cotton wool. All kinds of pictorial images are useful in this situation. Imagining that the note is a surfer, riding on the front of the crest of the wave has been a good image to use in Hawaii, for example. If the breath gets too far ahead of the tone, watch out! It is especially important that the teacher can demonstrate, and even exaggerate what the child is doing in a loving way, and then show a marked contrast when it is done correctly. Here is what Steiner has to say on the subject, in the lecture series *The Inner Nature of Music and the Experience of Tone*, although, of course, it must be converted into words that the child can grasp readily:

> *Imagine that someone stands on the ground. Surely the person can stand on it; otherwise he could not be there. You would not want to comprehend man, however, by the ground he stands on. Likewise, tone needs air for support. Just as man stands on the firm ground, so — in a somewhat more complicated way — tone has its ground, its resistance, in the air. Air has no more significance for tone than the ground for the person who stands on it. Tone rushes toward air, and the air makes it possible for the tone to stand.*
>
> *Tone itself, however, is something spiritual. Just as the human being is different from the earthly ground on which he*

stands, so tone differs from the air on which it rises. Naturally, it rises in complicated ways, in manifold ways.

Instrumental Lessons

It goes beyond the scope of this book, and well beyond my limitations, to comment upon which instrument a child should play. Clearly, one would never give a melancholic a flute, and while a sanguine might fall in love with the rich tone of the cello, the double bass, with its slow movement would not be suitable. Beyond such common sense observations, the choice of instruments is something for the class teacher and the music teacher to sort out.

Private instrumental lessons are best delayed until the child's musical being has developed enough to withstand the onslaught of conceptual study. (This does not apply to Suzuki methods and other teaching styles which focus on playing by ear.) Lessons should be actively encouraged once the child has passed fourth grade or so. The exception to this is the child who wishes to study trumpet and reed instruments. Here a delay is recommended, as any good teacher will tell you, because the diaphragm and air passages must have developed enough strength to withstand the pressure required to blow through the mouthpiece. Fourth or fifth grade is time enough for these instruments.

Anyone who has puzzled over what Steiner has to say on the subject of the dreaded piano as an instrument for study will perhaps remain silent when asked by parents of lower grade children – or suggest the lyre or harp, perhaps? Having made that qualification, I would think one could begin piano lessons in the middle school. Pianists are much highly valued and much in demand even in Waldorf schools after all, to accompany the eurythmy and chorus lessons!

Appendix B

Helping the "growlers" find the tone— Working with individual children

Over the years I have been teaching, I have met several individuals who "cannot sing." There are all kinds of terms for people who cannot accurately pitch their voices. Sometimes the person is not even aware they "can't carry a tune in a basket" and sing out lustily, at least a half-tone off the pitch that everyone else is singing, and sometimes they sit quietly while others around them sing, convinced that they are tone deaf. There's "something wrong" with them, and people have told them that they cannot sing, so they don't. Children, fortunately, are unaware of problems like this, in themselves or in their classmates during the early years at school, so there is time for them to mature enough to be singled out when at the age of ten or so, the teacher tactfully pulls them aside one day, "because I want to listen to you sing. You're doing something interesting when you sing, did you know that?"

After asking the young lady to listen carefully, sing a tone and ask her to sing the same tone. It may be that she has just not taken the time or made the effort to listen carefully in class, and the voices of her classmates have drowned out and confused the tone you have made at the start of each song. Most likely, though, the child simply has not learned what it feels like to "be in tune" with another person (this phrase has interesting associations).

Ask the child to sing a tone, any tone at all, or ask her to start a song that the class sings every morning. At the first note, join her on her note, whatever it is. She may look surprised, for this may well be a new feeling for her to be sharing the same tone as a neighbor. Let her change pitches, and lead you around, musically speaking, for a bit. Then using hand gestures to guide her, raise the tone by a step and ask her to follow you. Do this many times, going just a step or two above and below the original tone that she gave you. She will need to initiate the tone, which you then take up, and lead you about musically speaking many times before she will be able to find yours just from listening. Lots of praise will help bolster her confidence, too. By the second or third session you will be able to guide her to the tone you are singing, using hand gestures if necessary to help her get her bearings. I have found that usually the child becomes interested in this new experience and doesn't even mind it in class if you help her personally by giving a little "advice" coming round to stand near and using gestures in the singing lesson now and again. Her classmates will not tease her if you are subtle enough – they will be relieved more than anything, for sitting next to a "growler" is a trying experience for children.

Often the child, particularly if it is a boy, is locked into a speaking tone, deep in the chest, and the trick is to get him to find a higher, singing tone. This will have to be done with lots of humor and preferably away from any of his classmates. Try asking him to make a siren noise, or to howl like a wolf. (That's where the humor comes in. You will have to do it first!) Once he has got a good strong tone, join him on that pitch! From here on in the process, if it can be called that, is the same as for the child who just mumbles her way through the singing each day. The tone, however, must be refined and softened, and it will take a while for it to settle in and become a decent singing voice.

As I have said in the section on singing, sometimes one need do nothing but provide a good example in class of a singing tone with a clear, steady pitch. Over the course of several years, children who mumbled the lyrics of the class songs in grade one or two have found their voices by grade four with no extra help form the teacher but warm thoughts and encouraging smiles.

Appendix C

A suggested abbreviated music curriculum

Grade One

    Singing simple pentatonic tunes. The teacher sometimes uses hand gestures to indicate pitch. Preparatory finger exercises. The pentatonic recorder is introduced when the class is ready.

Grade Two

    Singing, with more defined pitch indications by the teacher, which can become games. Spoken, and clapping rhythm exercises. Drawing the "melody pictures" of some songs.

    Recorder continues on the pentatonic instrument, playing more complicated tunes. Pitch gestures of one or two notes as exercises on recorder. Rhythm exercises on one note, using picture-words.

Grade Three

    Singing can develop into simple rounds later in the year. Rhythm exercises continue, developing into rhythmic "rounds" as the year progresses, still using picture-words for the various note values, until the very end of the year. Singing the major scale. Introduction to the minor third in songs. Characterization and recognition of major and minor moods. Minor scales, if it is wished.

The **diatonic recorder** is introduced when the class is ready. The C major scale, finger exercises such as "the jump." The recorder played by imitation only. Later on, the D scale, if it is wished. Folk tunes are a good source for music.

The **Lyre**, an introduction to stringed instruments. The beginning **violin**.

Grade Four

Singing lessons once a week in the class, and another lesson each week as part of the junior choir. The interval exercises. Introduction to notation. Rhythm exercises introducing notation. More complicated rhythms to clap and rhythms in rounds. Part singing in choir, with the fourth grade usually reading the top voice, and music books to read from. Begin explaining the elements of a musical score.

Recorders: Identification of the notes of the scale and their pitch names. Point and play using the scale. Reading from the board. Simple harmonies. Reading later from individual sheets of music. Two and three part music on the soprano recorder. The teacher should begin to learn the alto fingering in preparation for teaching it in grade five.

Violin: the class continues to have violin lessons as a whole class. More technical skills are developed. As a transition from playing by ear to playing from a musical staff, the children learn the strings and fingering associated with each note in first position. Scales and point and play from the board. Use of a simple method book is certainly possible at this age. The direction and symbols for bowing. (The class bows in the air in unison while singing the melody of songs, for example.) Harmony in two parts.

Grade Five

Singing. The class continues in the junior chorus. Continuation of interval exercises and occasional testing to see that they are developing independent skills. More rapid progress in sight-singing is expected of them. Location of Do from the key signature and singing the scale names of the notes in simple pieces. More development of sight reading ability. One should expect them to hold their own part after two or three times through a piece in a chorus class, against the fourth grade's melody. "Ascending to Heaven" exercise, to refine tuning.

Identification of specific intervals and ability to sing the lower intervals (up to a perfect fifth) when asked.

Recorders. Introduction of the entire recorder family. I suggest that alto fingering be taught to the most musically able children, while the others continue to develop the soprano recorder and some switch to tenor. In a class of 25, five to six altos and three or four tenors with one bass would be a good balance. (See the text for grade five for suggestions on how to teach these different instruments.)

Strings: Introduction of the viola and cello for selected students. Reading music and scales and bowing exercises continue.

Musical tests can be given from time to time in all music lessons to ensure progress. A sample music test for fifth grade is included at the end of the recorder exercises. (See Ex. 13.)

Grades Six, Seven, and Eight

Main Lesson: In the Main Lesson, one can begin to form a "Class Orchestra," if wished, by inviting those who are playing violin, viola, and cello to take out their instruments each morning, but it is also good to continue to firm up the recorder skills. More complicated music in four parts. Expect most of the class to begin sight-reading on the recorder. Early music through Renaissance to Baroque music, for sight reading in class.

Continuation of **Strings** for select students, or for those who are studying privately.

Introduction of wind instruments as a new start for entering students or for those who sincerely wish to take up another instrument, or have not succeeded at strings. This is another chance to approach skills like fingering, sight reading, etc., on a new instrument.

Pick-up **recorder lessons** for those entering the school during the higher grades should be given at some point, and one could expect sixth, seventh, and eighth graders who have not managed to read properly earlier to wish to join. Class teachers can also send students. Perhaps a fee could be charged? In our school, this lesson meets in the afternoon after school.

Establishment of the **Upper Chorus** as a performing group, consisting for the sixth, seventh, and eighth grades.

The **Instrumental Music Lesson** is also in place two or three times a week, in which students from the sixth, seventh, and eighth grades are mixed together for musical study in **String Ensemble, Band, or Recorder.** (Other instrumental groupings could be included in this offering, depending upon the skills and interest of the teachers in the school. A **Renaissance Recorder Group** would be wonderful, or a **Guitar** or **Percussion Ensemble**, for example.) Musical skills continue to be developed in all groups. An **Orchestra** is also possible in these grades, if there are enough children who study orchestral instruments privately. For these grades and up, the school may need to hire a professional conductor. The children should have developed to a level beyond the teaching skills of an amateur, unless s/he is a very skilled musician.

High School

Orchestra and Chorus of performance quality is expected.

Exercises for Singing Lessons

1. Here is the rhythm exercise used throughout the lower school. One begins by having the children chant the words, leading over gradually in grade three and four to having them clap the rhythms. For rests, it is better to have them say Sh-h-h-h than just to remain silent. For eighth and sixteenth note rests, both on and off the beat, have the class mouth the word "rain-" or "-drop," and "Pitter (pat)- ter." These can be developed into quite complex rounds using different instruments for percussion in grades four and five.

2. Here is the first song I use for second grade to give the first indications of written music. We learn *Little Pony* thoroughly and use it at the start of each music lesson. We sing it all different ways: as gruff giants, as

sunbeams, as bubbles soaring high in the sky. Sometimes we just sing it over and over again, climbing a tone higher each time. The children walk the tune, stepping forward on the ascending notes and backward on the descending ones. We all use our hands to indicate the rising and falling pitch. Sometimes we "walk" the tune up our arm or along the desktop with our fingers.

Then one day I show them how it looks when I walk along and indicate the pitch. There are the hills of the song! Then I draw a simple picture on the board as I sing. The children get to do this at the end of the lesson. I have put the picture below and the song in musical notation. One would not show the children the notation, of course. Later, one can show the children where on the hills the notes are, because that is where the pony can carefully set his hooves down, and on the long notes, he stops to rest a bit.

LITTLE PONY

Little Pony, little pony, up the hill we go. Sometimes you are

very fast, and sometimes you are slow. If I walk a -long

be-sides, then perhaps we'll get there faster. Jumbo Joy, my pride!

Grade four and up

These are some of the exercises I have used with success at the start of each singing lesson, beginning with grade four. I try to add a new one every month or so, until the warm-up takes about fifteen minutes or so at the start of each lesson.

3. This is simply a scale followed by a major arpeggio. We begin on a convenient note (around middle C, but I usually don't pitch it so deliberately), and after the first scale, the whole exercise moves up a half step, and we continue to repeat that until we have gone as high as we can. Young children's voices are flexible. We usually go to two octaves above Middle C. Then we "climb back down" by using successively lower arpeggios until we can put two on top of each other, coming down to a low A or so for the bottom note:

doh re mi fa... ti do, do ti la...re do do do do, mi sol, do, sol me do...

4. This is the interval exercise. If a class sings this exercise several times a lesson for three years or so, they will never go flat! I have not dressed it up with any fancy pictures. It is important that the children learn the intervals by name as they sing them. Work with this exercise for a year or so, and then ask a grade five to characterize the intervals as you sing or play them. You will be amazed by their answers!

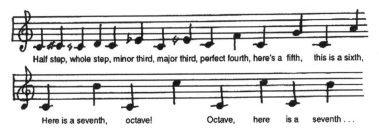

Half step, whole step, minor third, major third, perfect fourth, here's a fifth, this is a sixth,

Here is a seventh, octave! Octave, here is a seventh . . .

THE WHOLE SHEBANG

Half step, whole step, minor 3rd, major 3rd, perfect 4th, tri-tone, here's a fifth,

Minor sixth, major sixth, minor seventh, major seventh, octave! (+ down)

5. This one I have called "The Bumble Bee" for obvious reasons. It is fun, once the children know it well, if you have half the class "buzz" on the bottom note while the other half does the exercise. Then the parts switch. It can also be done in a round, with the second voice coming in a third later than the first, but "buzzing" is more fun and gets the children's nasal passages moving nicely. They can also experience their teeth buzzing as well if they hold their jaw so that the teeth are loosely touching.

Bumble Bee

Bumble bee – bumble bee – bumble bee bumble bee

bumble bee – bumblr bee – bumble bee – bumble BUZZ

6. "Bubbling" is a good exercise for placing the singing sound right outside the lips. Make sure the triplet rhythm is nice and even.

7. This one comes from the Sacramento Waldorf School. It is a great challenge to the fifth grade. The trick is to place all the half-step intervals so correctly that you actually do arrive at an octave on the top note! (Practice it yourself for a while first!)

8. This one we call "The Aria." The fourth and fifth grade love to do this. Make sure you "bounce" on the high note when you demonstrate it. They won't know it, of course, but it is a wonderful exercise for getting the diaphragm going in the proper way for singing. Place your hand over your diaphragm when you do it, and

you'll see what is meant. The movement is similar to what you feel there when you laugh or cough.

9. My class was thrilled by one exercise we did in grade five. They called it "going to heaven." Start with dividing the class and have them sing a third (Do and Mi) and the teacher adds the Sol. Then all of you go up, one half step at a time. I use my hands to signal when to rise each time. This is an excellent exercise in tuning carefully, as it takes constant adjustment to keep the chord in tune.

10. This melody is so beautiful that it can be used in many ways. The children might be able to include it later, after they have learned it, as an example of illuminated manuscript in their main lesson books in grade six. It would certainly be worth repeating as a musical experience in sixth grade, if it has been used already in the music lessons.

UT QUEANT LAXIS

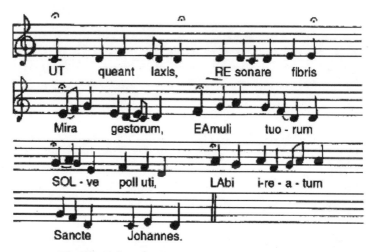

To "Build a Cathedral," the teacher divides the class into seven groups, with the seventh section being the largest. When the song is sung, group one sings only the first note, UT, and holds it while the rest of the class moves on through the piece. Group two stops when the lyrics reach the word **Resonare**, and holds the RE throughout the rest of the song. Group three "gets off" at MI and holds the tone; group four sing all the way until the FA of "famuli". Group five holds the SOL of "**solve**." Group Six holds the LA of "**labii** reatum." The last group, the largest of the seven, sings the song all the way to the end. During the singing of the last phrase, the earlier tones must get softer and softer until they fade away with the last note of the song.

Exercises for Recorders

11. This is "The Jump." Once you and the children have the pattern, use it for all the scales you learn. It is an excellent exercise for getting the fingers to stay in the right position and to cover the holes quickly.

THE JUMP

12. This exercise is called "Bubbling." It is more difficult than "The Jump," but it's quite pretty, and the class likes the challenge. Try this one in all the keys they have learned. One can use this all the way up the school.

Bubbling

Other exercises might be playing chromatic scales and minor scales in the later grades, along with all the above exercises in all keys.

A Musical Skills Test for Grade Five

Music Test

1. What note is this? Pitch name: _____
Scale name: _____

2. What note is this? Pitch name: _____
Scale name: _____

3. Does this bar have the correct number of beats? _____

4. Does this bar have the correct number of beats? _____

5. Give the pitches of these notes: _____

6. In the key of C, write the scale names: _____

7. The notes are all "doh." What should the key signatures be? Write in sharps and flats.

8. Row row row your boat . . . Write out the rest of the music in the key of C.

Endnotes

1 "*Now I ask you in all earnestness to compare what lies at the root of all these dreams. They have shown an acceleration and a fading away of feelings; tensions and, possibly, solutions; they have shown how the dreamer is irresistibly drawn towards a calamity, and so on. Compare this with what is fundamental in music and you will find in these dream pictures something chaotic, but nevertheless something which, in ordered form, belongs to the realm of music with its increase of tempo and volume, its fading-away and so on. ...People know so little about the origin of musical themes because their first-hand experience of them stems from the time between falling asleep and wakening. This is an element which has remained hidden in unconsciousness for the man of today, betraying itself only when weaving dream pictures. It is this unconscious element working through dreams — and in music through what belongs to melody — which we must try to get hold of in the art of education in order to overcome the harmful effects of the materialism in our time.*

If you compare the dreamy life of a child with an adult's world of dreams and also with the weaving of melodies in man, you will find a common origin. The child learns to speak unconsciously, as if waking from a deep sleep and finding himself in the realm of dreams. And melodies come, we know not whence. In reality they also emanate from the realm of sleep. We experience their plastic 'time-shapes' between falling asleep and waking, but man at his present stage of development is not capable of doing so consciously." Rudolf Steiner, **The Renewal of Education**, pp. 142-3.

2 Ibid., 143.

3 " *When we have reached the point after death when we lay aside the astral body, we also lay aside everything of a musical nature that reminds us of this life on earth. But at this cosmic moment music is transformed into the music of the spheres. We become independent of music experienced through the medium of the air and raise ourselves to another sort of music, the music of the spheres. . . .So in music and poetry we have an anticipation of what is our world and our existence after death.*" Ibid., p.67.

4 "*Whoever understands the human being from a musical aspect knows that sound, actual tones, are working within him. At man's back, just where the shoulder blades meet and from there are carried further into the whole human being, forming and shaping him, are those human forms which are constituted out of the prime or key-note. Then there is a correspondence in the form of the upper arm with the second, and in the lower arm with the third. And because there is a major and minor third — not a major and minor second — we have one bone in the upper arm, but two in the lower arm, the radius and the ulna; and these correspond to the major and minor third. We are formed according to the notes of the scale, the musical intervals lie hidden within us. And those who only study man in an external way do not know that the human form is constituted out of musical tones. Coming to the hand, we have the fourth and fifth, and then, in the experience of free movement, we go right out of ourselves; then, as it were, we take hold of outer Nature. This is the reason for the particular feeling we have with the sixth and seventh, a feeling enhanced by experiencing the movements of eurythmy. You must bear in mind that the use of the third made its appearance comparatively late in the development of music. The experience of the third is an inward one; with the third man comes into an inner relationship with himself, whereas at the time when man lived in the seventh he experienced most fully the going outwards into*

the world beyond himself. The experience of giving oneself up to the outer world lives especially strongly in the seventh." Rudolf Steiner, **Human Values in Education**, p. 150.

5 Rudolf Steiner, **The Arts and Their Mission**, p. 150.

6 *". . .All the possibilities of movement living in the limbs . . .are significant. These are immensely important for musical experience because dance movements are connected with musical experience. A large part of our musical experience is based on the fact that we have to restrain ourselves and hold back these movements. This indicates that musical experience is an experience of the whole human being."* Rudolf Steiner, **Art in the Light of Mystery Wisdom,** (London: Rudolf Steiner Press, 1970)p. 118.

7 *"As teachers we can work with this element (of melody) if we show our young pupils musical themes, if we analyse a simple melody as we would analyse a sentence. Already at a very early age we can let them experience a melodic theme like a spoken sentence. We can show the children where the tune begins and where it ends; or where, at a particular moment, the melody links on to the next part. We can say to them: Here is a kind of musical full-stop and here something new begins, and so on. To help children to become aware of a structure in a melody works wonders for their development. For thereby the child's attention is directed towards something external which, at the same time, is also part of human nature, but which is hardly ever noticed."* Rudolf Steiner, **The Renewal of Education**, p. 143.

8 Rudolf Steiner, **Art in the Light of Mystery Wisdom,** p. 43 and p. 21.

[9] Rudolf Steiner, *The Kingdom of Childhood*, (London: Rudolf Steiner Press, 1974), p. 112.

[10] Discover Magazine, "The Neural Orchestra," Josie Glausiusz, BrainWatch, September 1997.

[11] Rudolf Steiner, "The Human Being's Experience of Tone," included in the lecture series, *Art in the Light of Mystery Wisdom,* p.127.

[12] Rudolf Steiner, *Art in the Light of Mystery Wisdom,* (London: Rudolf Steiner Press, 1970), p. 118.

[13] Ibid., p. 164.

[14] Lea van der Pals, *The Human Being as Music,* (Stourbridge, England: The Robinswood Press, 1992), p. 29.

[15] Rudolf Steiner, *Practical Advice to Teachers,* (London, Rudolf Steiner Press, 1976), p. 49.

[16] Ibid.

[17] *"Regardless of man's relationship to rhythm, all rhythm is based on the mysterious connection between pulse and breath, the ratio of eighteen breaths per minute to an average of seventy-two pulse beats per minute. This ratio of 1:4 naturally can be modified in any number of ways; it can also be individualized. Each person has his own experience regarding rhythm; since these experiences are approximately the same, however, people understand each other in reference to rhythm. All rhythmic experience bases itself on the mysterious relationship between breathing and the heartbeat, the circulation of the blood."* Rudolf Steiner, *The Inner Nature of Music and the Experience of Tone,* p. 67.

¹⁸ It is interesting that the whole system of notation was "invented" specifically for the C major scale. The half-step intervals are inherent in our staff notation, and all the complexity of writing music (and playing it!) in different keys is complex mainly because of these inherent half-step intervals between E-F and B-C. I urge amateur music teachers to investigate how the different key signatures are built up - using a piano and the circle of fifths, it's fairly clear - to arrive at the order of the sharps. This structure of the major scale with its unbalanced yet dynamic pattern in its structure (whole step, whole, half, whole, whole, whole, half step) is a cosmic pattern, which Kepler found in the relationships of the orbits of the planets. Steiner describes the forms arising on a Chaladni plate in this way:

"The tone effects a distrubution of the material... When the spiritual tone of the celestial harmony sounded forth in the universe, it organized the planets into their relationships. What you see spread out in cosmic space was arranged by this creating tone of the Godhead." Rudolf Steiner, **Occult Signs and Symbols** , p.11.

¹⁹ Although in the passage quoted Rudolf Steiner was speaking of the curriculum as a whole, each music lesson is a little world of its own, and the balance which is needed in the overall daily rhythm is certainly neccessary in the music lesson:

"If a human being is occupied only with intellectual work, the process of the formation of carbonic acid is too strongly stimulated in him; the upper organism is saturated with carbonic acid. Now a proper, intelligently conducted musical education counteracts this excessive formation of the carbonic acid and enables the human being to bring again some activity, inner activity at least, into the carbonic acid process." Rudolf Steiner, **Deeper Insights of Education**, p. 41.

20 Rudolf Steiner, *Art in the Light of Mystery Wisdom*, p. 29.

2 Rudolf Steiner, *Occult Signs and Symbols*, p. 11.

22 Rudolf Steiner, *Waldorf Education for Adolescence*, p. 53.

23 Rudolf Steiner, *The Roots of Education*, p. 53.

24 Steiner speaks in harsh terms of the piano amost every time he mentions the instrument. In the section quoted in the text, he calls it a "kind of memorizing instrument." In other places he condemns it because the keys are all laid out in order of pitch in a quite artificial way. In one lecture, he calls it a "philistine instrument." He praised Bruckner's music because he said it made the piano disappear. Why such harsh words for the piano which stands enthroned in many, if not most musically cultured homes? I believe one reason is that with this instrument in particular, the player sits remote from the sounding strings, sits, in fact, almost motionless on a stool, quite far from the source of the musical sound. Between player and strings a complicated mechanism is hidden from view, consisting of purely mechanical moving parts- levers and hammers. When the student strikes the keys, he sets a complicated mechanism in motion. His movement is a percussive one, yet the result is melody as well as rhythm! Compared to nearly every other instrument, the pianist is quite removed from the musical experience of producing the tones. A violinist, for example must move her fingers to follow the melody as it sounds across the strings, and the bow must go where the melody takes it in lovely, arcing gestures, and the same is true of all wind instruments, the movement of

the body follows the flow of the melody, and breath and motion are engaged. This is a reflection of one's inner movement in singing, and indeed, even in listening to music being played. It is least present in piano playing, although the potential is there once the artistry has become great enough for the music to shine through.

25 Rudolf Steiner, "Lecture Three," *Three Lectures for Teachers*.

2 6 Rudolf Steiner, *Practical Advice to Teachers*, p. 49.

27 Rudolf Steiner, "Lecture Three," *Three Lectures for Teachers*.

28 Rudolf Steiner, *Balance in Teaching*, pp. 22-23.

29 Rudolf Steiner, *The Human Being's Experience of Tone*, p. 40.

Bibliography

Deighton, Hilda. *Singing and the Etheric Tone*, Gracia Ricardo's approach to singing based on her work with Rudolf Steiner, edited by Dina Winter. New York: Anthroposophic Press, 1991.

Glausiusz, Josie. "Neural Orchestra," Discover Magazine, BrainWatch, September 1997.

Goodwin, Joscelyn. *Cosmic Music*, Rochester, Vermont: Inner Traditions International, Ltd., 1989.

   Harmonies of Heaven and Earth, Rochester, Vermont: Inner Traditions International, Ltd., 1987.

Steiner, Rudolf. *Art in the Light of Mystery Wisdom*, London: Rudolf Steiner Press, 1970.

   The Arts and their Mission, Spring Valley, NY: Anthroposophic Press, 1964.

   Balance in Teaching, Spring Valley, NY: Mercury Press, 1982.

   Deeper Insights of Education, New York: Anthroposophic Press, 1983.

   "The Human Being's Experience of Tone," included in *Art in the Light of Mystery Wisdom*, London: Rudolf Steiner Press, 1970.

Human Values in Education, London: Rudolf Steiner Press, 1971.

The Inner Nature of Music and the Experience of Tone, Spring Valley, NY: The Anthroposophic Press, 1983.

The Kingdom of Childhood, London: Rudolf Steiner Press, 1974.

Occult Signs and Symbols, New York: Anthroposophic Press, 1972.

Practical Advice to Teachers, London: Rudolf Steiner Press, 1976.

The Renewal of Education, Forest Row, England: Kolisko Archive Publications for Steiner Schools Fellowship Publications, 1981.

The Roots of Education, London: Rudolf Steiner Press, 1982.

Three Lectures for Teachers, Stuttgart: mimeo graph 6/9/1919.

Waldorf Education for Adolescence, (Supplementary Course). Forest Row, England: Steiner Schools Fellowship Publications, 1980.

Van der Pals, Lea. *The Human Being as Music,* Stourbridge, England: The Robinswood Press, 1992.

Werbeck-Svardstrom, Valborg. *Uncovering the Voice,* London: Rudolf Steiner Press, 1980.